CONSCIOUS SOCIETY
Anthroposophy and the Social Question

CONSCIOUS SOCIETY
Anthroposophy and the Social Question
Eight lectures given in Dornach between 15 February and 16 March 1919

TRANSLATED BY MATTHEW BARTON

INTRODUCTION BY MATTHEW BARTON

RUDOLF STEINER

RUDOLF STEINER PRESS

CW 189

The publishers gratefully acknowledge the generous funding of this publication by the estate of Dr Eva Frommer MD (1927–2004) and the Anthroposophical Society in Great Britain

Rudolf Steiner Press
Hillside House, The Square
Forest Row, RH18 5ES

www.rudolfsteinerpress.com

Published by Rudolf Steiner Press 2018

Originally published in German under the title *Soziales Verständnis aus geisteswissenschaftlicher Erkenntnis* (volume 191 in the *Rudolf Steiner Gesamtausgabe* or Collected Works) by Rudolf Steiner Verlag, Dornach. Based on shorthand notes that were not reviewed or revised by the speaker. This authorized translation is based on the latest available (third) German edition (1989), edited by Robert Friedenthal

Published by permission of the Rudolf Steiner Nachlassverwaltung, Dornach

© Rudolf Steiner Nachlassverwaltung, Dornach, Rudolf Steiner Verlag 1980

This translation © Rudolf Steiner Press 2018

All rights reserved. No part of this publication may be reproduced, stored in a retrieval system, or transmitted, in any form or by any means, electronic, mechanical, photocopying or otherwise, without the prior permission of the publishers

A catalogue record for this book is available from the British Library

ISBN 978 1 85584 543 5

Cover by Mary Giddens
Typeset by DP Photosetting, Neath, West Glamorgan
Printed and bound by 4edge Limited, UK

CONTENTS

Editor's Preface ix

Introduction by Matthew Barton x

LECTURE 1
DORNACH 15 FEBRUARY 1919

The Paris Peace Conference and the Bern Socialists Congress; the social question: its solution must depend on far deeper foundations. The problem of laziness and comfort-loving in thinking, judgements based on mummified thoughts; the need for an understanding of the new. The appeal *To the German People and the Civilized World*; signatories being sought. The character of this appeal: not a programme but a pointer to forces at work in reality today. The war was only possible because no account was taken of real evolutionary needs when the empire was founded in 1871. The close connection between fantasy and 'pragmatism' (Ludendorff) must be overcome by grasping reality.

pages 1–16

LECTURE 2
16 FEBRUARY 1919

The need for social insights. The difference between the proletariat and its leaders, who are the inheritors of a bourgeois outlook. We need concepts commensurate with reality. Threefolding: not a system but something gained from observation of the deeper will of humanity. Real founding ideas, e.g. ground rent and subsistence minimum. The life of spirit and culture, the life of the state, and the life of the economy, and their relationship to pre-birth, earthly and after-death conditions. *Perception of God and Christ*. Harnack. Two paths to Christ: tolerance in thinking; self-acquired idealism in the will. Wilson's definition of freedom. The need to overcome the gentrified division between abstract culture and real life.

pages 17–35

LECTURE 3

21 FEBRUARY 1919

The social understanding we need must come from new, spiritual-scientific thinking. Modern, mummified, programmatic judgements in the social domain. Marx's form of thought: analysis of the conditions that have arisen in society but no productive ideas for the future. Taking thoughts to their ultimate conclusion. Radicalization of these thought forms by Lenin: the bourgeois state, taken over by the proletariat and perfected, will die away. Thoughts formed in accord with reality as it has been will lead nowhere. In relation to the future: 'social *ignorabimus*'. The two phases in Marxist-Leninist reform of society. The superstition that human renewal can come about through economic organization; failure to acknowledge the spirit. The need to overcome everything schismatic in spiritual science. The socialist faith in modern science; the need to emancipate it from narrow, bourgeois limits.

pages 36–54

LECTURE 4

1 MARCH 1919

The contrast between endeavours at the forefront of consciousness and in the depths of the soul: a materialistic view of history, the theory of class warfare and added value contrasted with the yearning for spiritual science, freedom of thinking and true socialism. The materialist view of history: a consequence of the materialism of gentrified science, art and religion. The true, spiritual sources of the five post-Atlantean cultural epochs. Class consciousness: a consequence of middle-class faith in the authority of the state; anti-state, international, but uniform; no individual awareness arising from freedom of thinking. The added value doctrine: a consequence of anti-social, bourgeois egotism. To understand added value as the foundation of cultural life, the proletariat must truly participate in culture. Threefolding of the social organism corresponds to humanity's deeper striving. Spiritual science must not become gentrified and schismatic. The Goetheanum building.

pages 55–70

LECTURE 5

2 MARCH 1919

Distortion of the real striving of the proletarian movement. J.G. Fichte as Bolshevik thinker in his *The Closed Commercial State*. Thinking born solely from the I cannot grasp and shape social reality. Fichte's *Theory of Scientific Knowledge*: a necessary stage in strengthening individual thinking before entering upon spiritual experience, but applied to sense reality it becomes destructive. Evil as distorted good. In the social realm: allowing hidden imaginations to take effect. Added value theory: masked untruthfulness in the relationship between employer and employee; the concept of commodity. Economic life and its relationship to natural foundations, on the one hand, and to the life of rights on the other. The true nature of the employment contract. Aspects of the relationship between economic life and the life of rights. Taxation legislation. Spiritual and cultural life, and also taxes to sustain them, must be founded on trust and freedom.

pages 71–86

LECTURE 6

7 MARCH 1919

Kurt Eisner. The necessity of understanding reality through spirit-oriented thinking. F. Mauthner; the difficulty of forming positive concepts of the state, which is a reversal of conditions in the world of soul and spirit. Earthly culture as a continuation of pre-birth life from residual antipathies. Economic life as the foundation for post-mortem sympathies. The loss today of a connection with the reality of spirit. Anti-social division between material life and a bourgeois existence that has grown decadent and luxurious. The worker's sense of being excluded. The need for a universally human education and culture, a new language in all fields. The Goetheanum building. The need to resort to primary, archetypal thoughts. The nature of money, which must be administered within economic life: capital. The healthy relationship between work and capital in the concord between free enterprise/initiative and the worker's free understanding, within a spiritual, cultural life in which both share.

pages 87–105

LECTURE 7

15 MARCH 1919

Modern thinking today refuses to learn from historical reality. J. Ude at the League of Nations conference. Modern thinking only encompasses the lifeless realm. Abolishing capitalism means destroying the social organism. A thinking that orientates itself to life must include the temporal aspect. Capital creation and its later reconfiguration in the threefold social organism. Gaining reality-attuned ideas by consciously raising oneself to imaginations. Organization of the head by the forces of the rest of the body from the last incarnation; tendencies which are consequently active in modern thinking. Reality-estranged thinking, e.g. Wilson's League of Nations idea of 1917 *after* the world war. The pacifist Schücking. World parliament based on the Weimar model. The basis for social renewal is a self-sustaining life of spirit and culture. The need to liberate the sciences from state supervision, which would also transform capitalism.

pages 106–118

LECTURE 8

16 MARCH 1919

Wilson's conditions for a League of Nations. The need to transform our thinking and integrate it with the social realm, but not without spiritualizing it. The emergence of socialist thinking from the thinking of the modern era. Fichte. Hegel's objective idealism: logic—nature—spirit; an organism of abstract ideas, but one relating only to the sensory realm, and excluding the real sphere of spirit (God, pre-birth life, post-mortem life). How Marx draws on Fichte, applying the triad of thesis—antithesis—synthesis to economic and material realities. Today a different trinity is needed: the human being between Lucifer and Ahriman; a human equilibrium between spirituality and materialism. *The Philosophy of Freedom*: a path to the reality of the spirit. The need today for an awareness of time. Socialization of thinking: empathy with all humanity. Cardinal Rauscher; Pobedonoszew. 'Historical obstinacy' and the need for new thinking to embrace what already lives today subconsciously in the world.

pages 119–134

Notes and references 135

Rudolf Steiner's Collected Works 141

Significant Events in the Life of Rudolf Steiner 155

Index 169

EDITOR'S PREFACE

These lectures, first compiled under the title *Die soziale Frage als Bewusstseinsfrage* were given to members of the Anthroposophical Society between 15 February and 16 March 1919, at a period of cultural and social chaos. These lectures formed part of energetic public efforts to cultivate social understanding and renew culture through innovative ideas relating to the threefold social organism. This period saw numerous public lectures held in the big cities of Switzerland, planning and launch of the appeal 'To the German People and the Civilized World', various attempts to contribute to the critical question of 'war guilt', transcribing and compilation of the book *Towards Social Renewal,* as well as the first public eurythmy performances in Zurich and Dornach. Hella Wiesberger chronicled Rudolf Steiner's activities in this period in the text 'Rudolf Steiners öffentliches Wirken für die Dreigliederung des sozialen Organimus. Von der Dreigliederungs-Idee des Jahres 1917 zur Dreigliederungs-Bewegung des Jahres 1919', published in two parts in the newsletter of the Rudolf Steiner Estate, no. 24/25 Easter 1969, p. 6-31, and no. 27/28, Michaelmas/Christmas 1969, p. 2–60.

INTRODUCTION

If we look around us at the physical world, its landscapes, buildings, roads, cars, bright lights, bridges, we see the tangible results of past human thinking and all the activity that has sprung from it. The same applies to our social institutions and the way we arrange, regulate, govern and perceive society. In other words, as Steiner says here, thoughts create reality, and so it is vital *how*—more so perhaps than *what*—we think. At this very moment, even if we think we are powerless to make a difference (and that belief is a thought too) we are helping create the world our descendants will inhabit. In the process we are either perpetuating old ideas, endlessly creating more of the same, or, perhaps painfully slowly, developing new ways of thinking and trying to act on them.

We can of course think anything we like, to the degree that we are self-aware enough not to succumb to inculcated ideas or misplaced faith in the authority of others. But once thinking has gone on to create its solid structures in the world, it seems hard to know how to change them radically without revolutionary chaos and attendant misery. The Marxist experiment, to which Steiner refers a good deal in these pages, did not have any fundamentally innovative ideas for reforming society. Rightly concerned at the plight of a whole downtrodden class of workers, it nevertheless had nothing to offer but an exchange of one autocracy for another, and it became clear that simply turning the tables on the aristocracy was not in itself sufficient to create a harmonious and healthy society. For Marxism, which picked up the baton of scientific materialism and ran with it, economics, and economic injustices, are paramount, the only acknowledged driving force and the root of all social malaise. While Marx and, around the time of these lectures, Lenin, had been giving workers a class identity and new outrage at the exploitation they suffered, rightly galvanizing them as a political force, they were also unwittingly feeding them only a materialistic view of the world, a 'surface ideology' that could not give them a deeper sense of their humanity and spiritual integrity. Everything pivoted on wages and economic power, on who held the reins of this power, and not on a deeper view of the very nature of the human being and what that view might lead to in terms of really new social structures.

Putting the human being, not just our economic activities, back at the centre of society, Steiner developed an incredibly subtle and discerning perception of how social dynamics could change and heal if they were founded on real insight into our threefold nature as individuals, social beings and economic participants in the world. The three, as he is always at pains to show, continually interact, but each is also a distinct 'sphere' in the same way that our single bodily organism can be seen, broadly, in terms of head, perception and thinking, heart, rhythm and feeling, and limb activity and will. Economics is therefore only one aspect of our human experience, which needs to be balanced against, and not swallow up, the very different needs and dictates of, on the one hand, human culture, art, religion and education, and, on the other, our legal equality as human beings, our inalienable rights. This tripartite thinking is very subtle because it recognizes that liberty, equality and fraternity are not universally valid principles in themselves but each only applies in *one* of these particular spheres.

Between the two extremes of revolutionary upheaval and a sermonizing Christianity, with its ineffective and status quo-maintaining code of ethics and exhortations, Steiner clears a truly middle ground and then starts exploring and expanding it. In the process he unfolds a vista of how past, present and future are at work within us—from which, if we grasp it, modes of social co-existence could develop that are truly innovative without being violently revolutionary. Striking is his insight that, with our narrowly materialistic perception of human nature and potential, we are all 'part of what's wrong', and that society will only change as we hone our own thinking and make 'perceiving reality' our 'inner soul practice'. Steiner, as he keeps reiterating, is not offering a programmatic agenda for change but a real foundation from which it can organically grow. Social forms and reforms, he says, are 'created together' not imposed by lone geniuses. Nevertheless, the detail of some of the thoughts and ideas he propounds here as a possible model for social thinking—down to the economic specifics of such things as commodity, labour, taxation, ground rent and capitalism itself—are staggering in their clarity and originality. This is no mystic effusion but a heartfelt plea, backed by profound insights, to change our thinking and therefore, in time, the world we ourselves must live in.

Matthew Barton

Lecture 1

DORNACH, 15 FEBRUARY 1919

The lectures I have given here recently[1] included a number concerning the social question that has come to be of such burning importance today. Unless we sleepwalk through events with which our own life is inextricably entangled, we will not fail to notice that this social question, as it has come to be called, really is of urgent and burning concern. You will be able to see from these lectures—some of which, in essence at least, I have also given as public talks in various places in Switzerland—that this social question has assumed a form very critical to the existential needs of modern humanity, and relates to all recent developments in human society. In our own circles, too, within the anthroposophic movement, a need has arisen to consider the destiny of humanity, as this relates specifically also to the social question, and to form judgements, drawn from our outlook, that could be turned into reality in the way in which we are capable of doing this.

For a long time now, some of our members have made efforts to place their strength in the service of these very difficult times in which we now live. In the process, various ideas and objectives have been pursued. It is of course true to say, my dear friends, that each person can only intervene in events in which he is destined to participate by his destiny, his karma, let us say by his place within humanity. The diverse aspirations that have arisen within our movement have led to the following: the three gentlemen who set themselves the task of working in Stuttgart in a way that addresses the existential need of our time, these three gentlemen whom you know well—Herr Molt, Dr. Boos, Herr Kühn[2]—came to see me at the beginning of February. We formulated the aim, as far as possible and useful, to realize in practice what we can draw from our outlook and worldview. Now my dear friends, when we are concerned not with reflections but with realities, it can only ever be a question of what is fitting and appropriate at a very particular time; what can be initiated in a particular respect and context. Not much will be gained usually by raging like a bull in a china shop. We have to make a tentative beginning in some way.

Given existing realities and precedents, it seemed to us appropriate firstly to do something that can at present seem the right course of action for the sorely burdened German people. If we look at current events, the first thing that strikes us—and I have often described this—is the chasm existing between different social classes: on the one hand what we can call the ruling classes as they have been up to now, and on the other the proletariat, the working classes who have been at the forefront of real demands relating to the social question. But a careful scrutiny will show that this proletariat appears in two forms: the proletariat as such, and then its leaders. I have often spoken here of the fact that all the ideas, feelings, aspirations and impulses which these proletarian leaders have in their heads, which gain sway over the working classes, are basically the legacy of the bourgeois thinking of recent centuries. We discussed these things from all kinds of angles, and have tried to consolidate our understanding of them.

But at the end of the day, we came back to the fact that a deep chasm does indeed exist between these social classes. In the last few days all of us will have been made aware, once again, of the depth of this divide: on the one hand Paris, where, based on their particular outlook, the ruling classes took in hand the fate of modern humanity;[3] and on the other, Bern,[4] with an assembly testifying to the chasm dividing its participants from those others. If you carefully followed what is emerging from Paris, as well as efforts being made at the Socialist Congress in Bern, you will have to acknowledge that the ideas and intentions issuing either from Paris or Bern are not the important thing. The thing that is really incisive for humanity's evolution in the long term is the fact that two radically divergent social languages are being spoken in these two places. If we are truly honest we have to acknowledge this: there are two completely different languages being spoken here, and no possibility of mutual understanding between them.

This phenomenon is so fundamentally important that anyone who properly reflects upon it must acknowledge what I have often said here: that we need to seek much deeper foundations than those usually sought if we are to understand what is at work here, and if we are to work towards possible solutions. As I said the day before yesterday in the public lecture in Basel,[5] the social question, the social movement, is of such pressing importance for a large swathe of civilization today, requires such urgent response, appears so incisive in historical terms, that it is hard to conceive of any previous time in humanity's history where things were as pressing. We need therefore to draw on deeper foundations. And, as I have so often suggested, we only find these deeper foundations in an outlook on reality which is the point of departure—also for studying social aspects of life—of our spiritual-scientific movement, of anthroposophically oriented spiritual science.

At our New Year gathering[6] I believe I pointed to something important: that one can certainly be very pessimistic about humanity, not only in some vaguer emotional way but based on a real appraisal of society. I read to you an essay by a man who is well qualified to make such an appraisal.[7] And then I said that such a sober and pessimistic outlook as he was expressing is nevertheless only possible if we are unaware of the help we can get by turning to the spirit. This awareness should become ever more widespread: that destructive forces, which will take dire effect in the forthcoming decades, can only be seen as inevitable if we refuse to turn to a view of reality that emerges from spiritual science. Of course I do not mean by this the dogmas of this or that spiritual movement; I mean in general the invoking of spiritual forces that, at this important turning point of humanity's evolution, are the only available wholesome and healing powers.

Thus we can say that one aspect of this anthroposophically oriented spiritual science will at the same time, in the most eminent sense, provide a cure for the ills of our era, since it does not issue from anything arbitrary but from true observation of the forces currently at work in the world. It really is not randomly conceived; it really is not a programme devised by one person or a group of people but has emerged from observation of what the spiritual guidance of the cosmos itself dictates as a necessary influx into humanity's current development. This alone allows us to speak as we do of anthroposophically oriented spiritual science—for otherwise it would be arrogance to do so. But what originates, in fact, from honest humility, need not fear the foolish objections it meets with, as it seeks expression, from those who label it arrogance.

From Paris, we can say, issues all that is borne on the grandiose wings of an outlook that has clearly led to absurdity over the past four and a half years. From Bern has issued something that a number of people regard as a remedy but which does not draw on a deep enough source. From Paris there issues something that alarms almost all of humankind; from Bern came something a great number of people pinned their hopes on. These two things still speak a completely different language, and there is no communication across the chasm dividing them. This communication will only become possible when the soul seeks to appeal inwardly to spiritual science.

It was this that gave rise to the thought of reaching out to one part of humanity at least, seeking its understanding. For understanding is what is required. I have repeatedly stressed that we will make no headway in the chaos in society without first gaining understanding from a sufficiently large number of people in the civilized world, and doing so before instincts start to run rampant. This is also what underlay the spirit of my lectures in Zurich, Bern and Basel. What I have continually discussed with various people recently is how we can appeal to people's understanding, and whether it is even possible at all to count on some degree of understanding before a full-scale debacle breaks out. Now this latter question is not in fact one that we can ask if we are in tune with reality, for then we do not establish hypotheses about what may or may not be possible but instead we take the measures we consider necessary. When we embark on a path we have to take the first step. And we should not think, if this first step does not immediately appear to be identical with the desired goal, that it should therefore be discounted. After all, the first step on a long journey can only ever cover a very small part of it. All that matters in aiming for a particular goal is that we do not start by heading in the opposite direction, or deviate to left or right; and secondly that we maintain the will to persist in our intent, once we have embarked on it, and do not allow ourselves to be pushed to left and right by all the obstacles we might encounter. Besides this, if we wish to root ourselves in reality we have to relate to actual contemporary conditions, to what exists, and not build castles in the air. Our ideas have to relate to something already manifest, already present as a real tendency. It can sometimes actually seem as if our first step were a very hapless one, and it may only become clear that it is not after we have gone a little further down the road.

When these three gentlemen, Molt, Boos and Kühn, came to discuss these things with me, firstly we had to ask—since after all a spiritual impulse was necessarily involved, and an appeal to people's insight—what, in our experience, meets with a response from human thinking. You will recall the 'Appeal to the Civilized World' (well, the supposedly civilized world) made once by, I think, 99 professors, people well-known in Germany.[8] If we judge according to reality rather than simply out of emotion, we are likely to consider this appeal to have been extremely inept. Well, of course most of them were professors. Nevertheless, it made an impression, it found its way into people's minds in a very unfortunate manner. And the effects still echo on today. In some respects it was a reality, one that contributed more to the downfall of the German people than many other things. It created waves.

And so this thought occurred: how would it be now, at a time when things are so desperate, to counter this sum of ideas that were issued back then, were unleashed on humanity—ideas that were blatantly outmoded—by doing something to nurture communication and understanding: an appeal to humanity drawn now from real, existing conditions? Initially, as seems self-evident, this appeal would be directed to the German people whose destiny it has been to see its supposed task swept away along with its whole legislature. One could initially appeal to this German nation, pointing out what realities themselves make plain—not mere words, judgements and thoughts, but facts and realities. While such an appeal might be addressed in vain to a great part of humanity, because the old frameworks still survive, it is conceivable that the German people would hear it, since their old foundations have simply been pulled from under their feet. They might recognize that the old certainties no longer sustain them but that a new basis must be found for their task in the world. That is how people are, after all: as long as the old sustains them a little—even if they change their outward garb—they cling to old customs and ignore everything that is telling them they can't actually go on clinging to it any longer. You have scarcely any idea what a role comfort plays in the inner life of humankind.

Well, with these thoughts in mind, my dear friends, I wrote a kind of manifesto,[9] which I think might be heard by souls who, in respect of the question of our culture, are open to communication founded on a healthy ground of reality. I think it might be understood, initially, by insightful people in the German nation, to whom it is specifically directed. But it also seems to me that it should be read by enemies of the German people—as something that can be seen at present as appropriate for this German nation to consider and realize. In view of the fact that the earlier appeal I mentioned was signed by 99 people, I thought it might be good if once again we could find another 99 within the boundaries of German Germany, of former Germany, of former Austria; and that perhaps these 99 might be joined by a small number of others in neutral countries—particularly in Switzerland—who are open to understanding present existential needs. If all this were possible, it seemed to me, we might achieve something positive to redress the previous negative influence of those other 99 figures.

I hope you will understand me aright! The appeal is first and foremost addressed to the German nation. But what is aired in this way within the German nation should also be heard throughout the civilized world. I will now read the appeal. The ideas it contains will be familiar to you, my dear friends, since we have often discussed them. Of course they can be only briefly expounded in this succinct form. The aim here is not to instruct anyone but to say something that can point people's attention to the existence of a way forward, and to the right way of embarking on it. Naturally some may object to the brevity of this appeal. Yet it is not a manual but merely a pointer to the fact that there are sources of help within humanity. Here it is.

To the German People and the Civilized World

The German people believed that the edifice of their empire constructed half a century ago was assured forever. It seemed to them in August 1914, at the outset of the catastrophic war, that this edifice would prove invincible. Today they gaze upon its ruins. Such experience—given that it has shown half a century's beliefs, and especially the prevailing outlook of the war years, to be a tragic error—must be followed by self-reflection. What were the causes of this fateful error? This question must inevitably lead to long and deep self-examination by the German people. Their capacity to survive and develop will depend on whether they can find the strength for such self-examination. Their future depends on whether they can truly take this question to heart: how did I succumb to this error of mine? If they can ask this question of themselves today, it will dawn on them that half a century ago they founded an empire and yet omitted to assign it a task that sprang from the intrinsic nature of German culture, of the German people. An empire was founded; and in its early period, efforts were made to organize its living inner potential in accordance with the needs arising from year to year from both old traditions and new demands. Later this changed, so that instead an outward sway and power rooted in material forces was consolidated and enlarged, connected with measures relating to the social demands emerging in the new era. While these measures did take some account of much that arose as current necessity, they lacked the larger vision that should have arisen from insight into the developmental powers toward which modern humanity must turn. Thus the empire was embedded in a world context without having an essential goal that justified its existence, and this became sadly apparent as the catastrophic war unfolded. Before the outbreak of the war, non-German countries of the world could have seen nothing in the conduct of this empire that might have suggested that those governing it were in any way fulfilling a world-historical mission, one that ought not to be brushed aside. Its failure to find such a mission inevitably led to the view amongst other nations that, for people with real insight, is the deeper cause of the German collapse.

For the German people, an immeasurable amount now depends on their unprejudiced assessment of the situation. Misfortune should lead to insights that people refused to contemplate in the previous fifty years. In the place of a small-minded appraisal of the needs arising as we move into the immediate future, we need a broad survey of the developmental powers at work in modern humanity, a strength of mind to try to perceive them and to dedicate ourselves to them with courageous will. We must overcome the petty view that all who focus on these developmental powers are useless and impractical idealists. The time is over for the pride and arrogance of those who think they are pragmatists and yet whose narrow-mindedness, masquerading as practicality, has led to this misfortune. It is high time to recognize what those decried as idealists—who are in fact the truly practical ones—have to say about the developmental needs of the modern era.

For a long time now the 'pragmatists' of all persuasions have seen quite new needs arising for humanity but they sought to accommodate them within the framework of old, traditional habits of thinking and institutions. Modern economic life has led to these needs and demands, and it seemed impossible to satisfy them by means of private initiatives. *In specific fields*, one class of people thought it imperative to lead private labour over into social labour; and this was brought about in the areas that this social class deemed profitable to it. It became the goal of a different social class to radically transform *all* individual labour into social productivity. Contemplating the development of modern economic life, this latter class had no interest in preserving the old private goals.

All efforts that have so far emerged to meet the needs of modern humanity share one thing in common: they seek socialization of the private sector and count here on communal bodies (the state, local government) taking this over. Yet these bodies originate from conditions that have no connection with the new needs and demands. Alternatively, people count on newer types of association (such as collectives or cooperatives) that were not directly founded to meet these new demands but which have been created in the image of the old forms, through traditional modes of thinking.

The truth is that no communal institution created in line with these old modes of thinking can be a proper vehicle for what is now necessary. The times urge us to discern a social structure for humanity that takes account of factors very different from those usually considered. Hitherto, social communities have largely arisen through humankind's social instincts. It is the mission of our era to bring full consciousness to bear, now, on the powers at work in society.

The structure of the social organism is like the natural organism of the human being. And just as our heads and not our lungs are responsible for thinking, the social organism must be articulated in different systems none of which can be taken over by another, each preserving its autonomy while at the same time interacting and collaborating with the others.

Economic life can only thrive if it develops as an independent element of the social organism in line with its own forces and laws, rather than being brought into disarray by the invasion of a different sector of the social organism, that of politics. This political element should instead exist in full autonomy alongside the economic realm, just as, in the natural organism, the respiratory and head systems exist alongside each other. These would not function in wholesome harmony if governed by identical laws, and likewise politics and economics must each be administered by their own laws and systems of management, albeit in living interaction with each other. This is because the political system will inevitably destroy the economy if it seeks to take it over, while the economic system loses its life forces when it seeks to become political.

Then a third element must join these two sectors of the social organism, once again in full independence and formed in accordance with its own living potentiality: that of spiritual or cultural productivity. This third realm at the same time encompasses the spiritual portion of the two other spheres, supplying this to them out of its own intrinsic laws and manner of administration. Once again this third sphere cannot be controlled or influenced except as happens in the mutually influencing parts of a natural organism.

What has been said here of the requirements of the social organism can already be fully substantiated and developed in all details. In these comments we have only established the general principles involved for all who wish to pursue these vital matters further.

The German empire was founded at a time when these imperatives started to arise for modern humanity. Its government failed to understand how to shape its task in accordance with these imperatives. If it had done so, this would not only have given the empire the right inner constitution but would also have lent justification to its outward policies; and through these the German people could have lived harmoniously with other nations.

Now disaster can help us gain insight. We need to develop the will for a potential social *organism*. The other countries of the world ought not to find a void where Germany once was; instead three systems, with three autonomous delegations—cultural-spiritual, political, and economic—should negotiate with those who vanquished the *one* Germany, a nation which, through disarray and confusion of the three systems, became an impossible social structure.

One can just imagine the 'pragmatists' objecting vociferously to the complexity of what has been said here, and finding it hard even to contemplate the collaborative interplay of three entities, because they have no desire to acknowledge life's actual demands, instead trying to shape everything in line with the comfortable dictates of their *own* thinking. They will have to recognize that there are only two alternatives: either to submit our thinking to the demands of reality or to learn nothing from misfortune, and thus infinitely multiply the dire scope of what has already occurred.

*

The three gentlemen I mentioned have now set off for Germany with this appeal, and while I have been giving my lectures here in Zurich, Basel and Bern, they have been trying to realize what we envisaged: to find near enough a hundred signatories. Herr Stein[10] took on this task for Austria, while other people have been undertaking similar efforts here in Switzerland.

Well, there hasn't been much time yet, but we can be very pleased at the response so far to this first step: we have launched an appeal supported in the same way as that hapless earlier one. At my latest lectures in Zurich—held quite intentionally in Zurich since Switzerland is currently the fulcrum of all international events—my aim was to show that there are people, here and there, with dawning understanding of these things. And naturally therefore I wanted to hear the outcome before I gave the last Zurich lecture. It was very pleasing to learn that we had obtained a hundred signatures so far, excluding Switzerland and Vienna. I was informed of this on the 11th already. This news reached me from Germany where our friends had left no stone unturned to achieve it. On the same day, the 11th, at midday, I received a telegram from Vienna saying they had obtained seventy-three signatures, and would assuredly get more the following day—which indeed turned out to be so: 93 by the next day. Herr Stein sent me this news. And then a further number of signatures were added retrospectively. The results so far, therefore, have been very satisfying. And it would be welcome, now we have got this far, if a number of people—including well-known figures, people whose view is respected, since this is important in such a campaign—would publish such an appeal wherever this can be done, so that it is seen, read and comes to the attention of those for whom it is intended. Actually it concerns everyone in the world today. It is true to say that something lives in the depths of human souls that draws them towards understanding of such concerns.

In the course of these lectures I have said that the idea now manifesting in this form is not a new one of mine.[11] Back at a decisive turning point in this catastrophic war, I was trying to help realize this necessary impulse in the places where I could. I described to you how this came about. Back then I was telling those to whom these things needed to be addressed that this is not a programme, not an ideal, but rather something observed and observable in terms of developmental forces in modern humanity—something seeking definite realization in the next ten, twenty or thirty years. It cannot be a matter of whether or not it comes to pass but only how it does so. And I said to quite a few key figures back then that they had the choice either to pursue a rational course in order to realize something like this, or to witness social cataclysms and revolutions. It did not take long for people to recognize that this was no false prophecy. But comfort-loving folk today find it hard to move on from a certain understanding to developing the courage necessary to make such things reality, in so far as their position allows.

Here in Switzerland a few signatories have been found too, but there is a concern here—given that the first part of the appeal speaks of the need for the German people to examine themselves, and reflect on the error in which they were entangled—that it might not be the place of the Swiss to tell the Germans what to do. But in my view, dear friends, this reservation is no longer appropriate. As old, mummified ideas, such concerns may have had some significance prior to 1914, but they no longer do so today. Nowadays there is no place any more for the pettiness reflected in this kind of national reserve. The last, disastrous four and a half years have surely taught us this. It is high time to think differently—forgive me—even in

Switzerland, from the way people thought just four and a half years ago. Here too, people should have learned something if they have observed the last four and half years with any acuity. This brief period can appear to us like centuries. And it is almost beyond belief when the old, national prejudices, and other such preconceptions, old, mummified ways of thinking which should really have ended in 1914, are thought to be the right foundation for a new world order, a new map of Europe. This European house of cards will quickly collapse when shaken apart by the other forces, the social realities which alone hold sway today and are the sole determining factors in what is called politics. Everything else just masks this reality. And the Europeans will be sorely mistaken if they try to judge things, and object to things, in terms of the old, habitual modes of mummified thinking.

Of course it can be said—and I could easily give you a compendious account of all the refutations—that this appeal is a proposal for all countries to adopt, and could only come about if they all made a start on it. No, my dear friends, a single 'state' can make a beginning. The proposals are perfectly well suited to that. And if one country does so, it has done something for the benefit of all mankind. It was the German people's misfortune that their empire was founded in a phase of modern history, at a time when it had become necessary to inform it with this mission. Because this mission was not embraced, other nations could not understand what on earth it was doing, what its *raison d'etre* was. If it had adopted and pursued this mission, all events would have taken a different course: its existential justification would then have been apparent and palpable.

Nowadays people's thinking and judgements are trapped in mummified ideas. You see, there are a great number of people in Europe who cannot free themselves from their old, mummified ideas about Europe; and yet at the same time their fear leads them to regard the world grandee Wilson[12] as some kind of—well, I'm not sure how to put it—as a redeemer. But people ought to refrain from their views of Wilson before ascertaining how he became so influential in his country. He did so out of his healthy American instinct, precisely by combating all the other parties with a politics diametrically opposed to what a great part of Europe now wishes to slide into. A great portion of Europe wants to sail into a community, a social community politics, in which the freedom of the individual, each person's distinct powers, will go under. Wilson owes his election, and his influence, solely to the fact that, as an American Democrat, he helped unleash the individual forces embedded in the economy. Let us hypothetically assume that Europe were to achieve the ideals of Bolshevism, the ideals of Bernese social democracy—I mean the social democracy of the Socialist Congress that took place in Bern. If we assume this were realized, that people achieved these dreams of theirs, then Europe would become a configuration from which—despite all national prejudices—all powers of freedom would necessarily drain away to free America, where Wilson himself came to power through precisely the opposite. Terrible competition would develop between Europe and America, and this would inevitably lead to Europe's impoverishment and the enrichment of America: not because of injustice but due to the idiocy of socialist politics in Europe. This is what would happen if, in Europe, we do not conceive and realize social forces in a way that corresponds to the healthy social organism—which is precisely the task of European humanity.

This appeal is not something that has simply been conceptually elaborated but it points, rather, to powers everywhere at work in reality, powers that must be realized and without whose realization not only the fate of Germany and Austria but of all Europe too must truly succumb to impoverishment, misery and unspirituality.

We live at a grave time in which small-mindedness will not suffice. Something lives in people themselves, too, which draws them to what is expressed in this appeal. That is an observable fact. And because this is so, because we may harbour hope that we can reach people's hearts and souls, an attempt has now been made to reshape what we tried to do during the war, in the way appropriate then, and adapt it for current conditions.

I hope, though, that no one will think that these proposals are intended as absolute. In January 1918 I spoke of them to a gentleman who later became a key figure,[13] in the terms in which they were couched at the time; but I told him that they could of course always assume different forms in accordance with changing conditions. This is because they are not theoretical, not a programme or ideal, but are conceived and drawn from reality. And I said, furthermore, that because of this I was not pursuing a course such as that of many utopians. Utopian programmes are based on the idea that they must be realized as formulated, and that things will go badly otherwise. But this is not my aim in the slightest. It may be that such a proposal makes an impression on people and that, because it is practically conceived, they begin to realize it in practice. In any and every field of life today one can say very clearly already how a beginning can be made with practical implementation. But I could also imagine that nothing, not a single stone, might remain of what I have said here, and also in my lectures in Zurich, Bern and Basel; that everything might assume a different configuration. If your thinking corresponds to reality, it does not matter that your formulae, your principles, are realized but that somewhere in reality they are grasped, taken hold of. What emerges from this will become apparent, and that is the important thing. Everything might develop in a different way—I want to make clear that this is absolutely possible; but certainly what will emerge will be appropriate to actual circumstances. Rather than an abstract ideal, some programme, these proposals encompass forces of reality, as far removed as possible from all fantasy, and equally all dry theory. That is why I was so astonished when someone widely spoken of,[14] whom one of these three gentlemen assumed would also be a signatory of this appeal, sent me a message expressing his surprise that an appeal written by me did not appeal more to the spirit of humanity; did not state that humanity could only find its salvation by finding a way back to the spirit.

You see, people want you to keep repeating and reiterating the word 'spirit'. But that is not the important thing. What is important is that the spirit manifests, that it shows itself able to really shape realities. The greatest harm is done by those who continually speak of 'spirit' without seeking to pinpoint its reality. They are talking ideologically, not spiritually. And we should be thankful, my dear friends, that from within our society have emerged people with real understanding—and willing to actually act on it—of what is intended here. And this elicits a response.

After my last lecture in Zurich, when I referred to this appeal arising as an outcome of our deliberations, our friend Dr Boos issued his own appeal to the gathering, calling for a number of volunteers willing to undertake practical action in this matter. The result was extremely pleasing. Naturally some made objections, and I can well understand them. But the nature of such objections shows that people today are not rooted in reality but are fervent dreamers. Actually those regarded as the greatest pragmatists are fantasists of this kind. That is why I said in a lecture in Zurich that General Ludendorff[15] himself is a fine example and embodiment of a modern fantasist: a person who acted strategically for better or worse—and in my opinion worse—but in relation to everything else was far removed from a grasp of life and reality. Exerting great influence, more is the pity, he was far removed from reality and had no inkling of the real conditions within which he should have acted: an abstract idealist in the same way as any socialist utopian. It is high time that people took a long, hard look at this highly dubious term, 'pragmatic', which has caused endless mischief amongst humanity. This pragmatism is really nothing other than fantasy brutally implemented in reality, an unreal mode of thinking; and it is high time this were abandoned. That's the important thing, my dear friends. What is needed instead, what must come, is what springs from the spirit of the anthroposophically oriented movement—as does this appeal, which has emerged from the heart of our movement, and which I wanted to tell you about this evening as part of our series of lectures.

LECTURE 2

DORNACH, 16 FEBRUARY 1919

I keep reiterating[16]—and did so again yesterday in connection with our appeal—that my priority in the life and context of modern humanity is to elicit true social understanding in as many people as possible. It must not be forgotten that the conditions that have developed in recent times have brought a kind of chaos over a large swathe of the civilized world, and that the only remedy for this chaos will arise within human souls themselves. External measures—whether these are conceived as legislature or as merely external organization of economic life—will not prove capable of properly and comprehensively aiding humanity in the situation that has now arisen. In some lands, certainly, things can continue as they are for a while, but it would be mistaken to believe that, faced with the social inundation inevitably swelling now and threatening to overwhelm all humanity, isolated countries can preserve their status quo in the long term. No aid can come other than from social understanding and insight, from ideas developing within human souls about social conditions.

What I have now said in a somewhat complex fashion can also be said more simply: what is driven into disorder will not come back into order unless people show themselves able to create order. And they will only do so if they acquire real social understanding, something that humanity today—and people of all political persuasions—are very far removed from indeed. The first thing to be considered is how to spread this social understanding. Here it is of overwhelming importance that what lives in the souls of millions and millions of proletarian workers is at odds with what lives in the ruling classes. The governing classes bear within them, very largely, the legacy of a gentrified outlook, and seek to apply this now, albeit in somewhat campaigning fashion, to the conditions in which the workers live.

This is a drastic reality, one we only take proper account of by resolving, firstly, to disseminate social understanding. Even if it is clear that outward conditions are likely to become still more confused than they already are, it would be mistaken to think that anything will be gained by patching them up at critical places. What is generally lacking today is social insight, and it is lacking because the whole development of thinking, of feeling and will too, in modern times, has been alien to the development of social understanding. Even those who carry a powerful social impulse today have extraordinarily little social insight.

But please do not imagine that social insight depends on some esoteric, wide-ranging, comprehensive knowledge. Rather, the most elementary social orientation is lacking in people today. People think in terms quite other than those needed to acquire the most primitive social understanding—which is all that is required to start with. The right course, above all, is to seek a path that leads away from the abstract, fantasist ideas that many today so comfortably adopt. People believe that it is possible today to solve the social problem from some ethical or religious perspective, but this is not so. Preaching ethical and religious sermons warms the heart and has some, especially egoistic, effect, but what is actually needed is to render our ideas capable of intervening in the fabric of society itself.

So much depends today, therefore, on acquiring social insight. I said that even those who bear a powerful social impulse often have primitive ideas. There are many people, aren't there—belonging both to the ruling classes and to the working classes—who think that a simple reordering of the classes can bring about real change: for example, if those who have been dominant, ministers and secretaries of state, are demoted while others previously in lower, working-class positions, rise to the top. It would be completely mistaken to think this. Many may deny that they harbour such ideas, and yet they do. They are befuddled by all kinds of partisan views and so are unaware that this is what they really think. What is needed is quite simple. People need to develop understanding of what I have often presented both here and in public lectures: understanding of the necessary threefolding of the social organism. All aspects of social measures need to be undertaken in a way that takes account of the necessity implicit in this threefolding. That's the important thing. Whether such measures relate to, say, building a railway that is to be assigned either to a private company or to the state, or whether it is a matter of remuneration for work accomplished—and I specifically do *not* say remuneration for an employee—in all these matters the measures taken should accord with this threefolding principle, in line with the independence of, respectively, spiritual life, the life of rights—the state, political life *per se*—and economic life.

People may well ask how one thing or another should be done, but mostly such questions are mistaken at the stage in which we now are with these matters. The spirit of what lives in this threefolding movement can be described roughly as follows. To take just one instance, let's consider the taxation system. At present it is not a matter at all of conceiving the best possible taxation system but instead of working towards threefolding. And as this is increasingly realized, the best tax system will naturally develop via the action of this threefold social organism. We have to create the conditions under which the best social institutions can emerge. It is no good for someone to sit down and fabricate the 'best system', for this will have no value in reality. Even if you were the greatest genius who ever lived and could conceptually elaborate the best taxation system possible, it will serve no purpose if others reject it. Maybe what they want is wrong, but they do not want what you propose. That is the important thing. So it isn't a matter of conceiving the best system but of discovering what can form the soundest basis on which all humanity will do the best it can. And then you might say: yes, but one has to start somewhere. One has to establish threefolding even if people don't wish it!

But here we are in a different realm, not one where people either wish or don't wish a particular tax system. Here we are concerned with something that basically all people desire once they understand it. If you find the right way to do so, this is something you really can get people to understand, for subconsciously human beings desire its realization throughout the civilized world in the next few decades. This is not something theoretical but an observation of what human beings intend. Numerous people reject it at present not because they do not want it but only because they are full of preconceptions and are still really working counter to something that seeks realization. We have to focus on the thing of underlying, primary importance. Understanding can awaken for the primary thing here—however long it takes—if some of what impedes understanding is removed. Naturally some in the ruling classes still stand in the way of this. It will be impossible to persuade them, and they will never come round until they get a bloody nose from all the resistance they encounter. There will be a great deal of such resistance. And that is why, if we do not at first succeed in the way we imagine, we should not give up on this approach and think it in vain. Preparation is needed for this outlook, which must be waiting in the wings when what is at present—mistakenly—being realized in the world has led to absurd extremes; and when much of what is figuring in the world has gone like say, the German princes, who in 1913 never dreamed that they would be gone by 1919. When everything that people still praise to the skies has vanished, something at least must remain in their hearts and minds which they can resort to. This must be prepared. The ground must be laid. This is the view you should hold to my dear friends. Once you have delved deep enough and for long enough into this threefolding of spiritual life, political life and economic life, you will experience a need to develop further understanding of these matters. It is this understanding that is so much needed, otherwise people talk about everything with the best will in the world but no reality can ensue from it. The social organism is subject to certain laws in exactly the same way as the natural human organism. If, however fine your principles, you act counter to these laws of the social organism, you will achieve nothing. At most you will lead people down a cul-de-sac. This is the important thing.

Do not imagine it contradicts human freedom to be placed into the fabric of a social organism with particular laws. This is not a sensible thought. We might equally well ask whether we are free because we are compelled to eat every day. Eating or not is not part of our freedom. The things in the world that are subject to a certain lawfulness, in which we are embedded, have not the least to do with the problem of freedom, any more than our inability to reach up and pluck the moon down to earth has anything to do with our freedom. Something else is connected with the social understanding that we need: our capacity to delve back into fundamental, primary matters and not hang our social insight upon secondary or tertiary things, which are only an after-effect. Of course, in certain respects we can say that we need a minimum value to subsist—and let us directly translate value into monetary terms here: we need a certain income to survive. In certain respects we can speak of a minimum livelihood. But in speaking of this minimum livelihood we can be referring on the one hand to something completely self-evident and yet on the other to something that is utter nonsense. Let me try to illustrate what I mean with an example.

If you study conditions in a particular region, a basic feeling, an instinctive feeling can perhaps tell you that someone who does simple, manual labour, requires so and so much as minimum livelihood, otherwise he cannot live in his community. This may seem a self-evident thought. But ask yourself now if it is equally self-evident when, in the terms I have stated, this is unrealizable within the social organism within which someone lives; if this simply can't be realized. What then? This is the question that must be addressed first and foremost—what happens when it is impossible for this to be realized?

Matters as I just described them are not a primary thought. People do not go back to fundamentals but start from secondary things, mere after-effects of others. To gain social understanding we must always seek to return to first things. One fundamental thing here is to be able to form a view, a life-enhancing view, of how the minimum livelihood can arise in accordance with the living, determining realities of the social organism. By life-enhancing I mean, in this case, a view or outlook from which tenable social conditions and a tenable social community of people can ensue. That is the primary thing. But now we arrive at certain ideas that modern humanity may often find very uncomfortable since, in the last few centuries, education has failed to address them or direct people's attention to them in a meaningful way. It is high time that people realized that to be halfway educated involves more than knowing that three times nine is twenty-seven. It is equally important to understand the meaning of a term such as 'ground rent'. Let me ask you this: how many people today have a clear idea what this means? And yet without seeing how such things form part of the social organism, it simply won't be possible for humanity to prosper in future.

These things have gradually become very confused. And this confusion has led to people formulating ideas that do not reflect actual conditions in this realm. You see, the ground rent that can be evaluated according to the productivity of a certain piece of land gives rise, let us say, to a particular sum for a state-defined region. Land is worth so and so much according to its productivity, or in other words according to the manner or degree of its rational exploitation in relation to the overall economy. For people today it is very difficult to think of this simple land value in clear terms, because in a modern economy capital interest or capital in general has become confused with ground rent. This is because the real economic value of ground rent has been falsified by mortgage law, bonds and stocks trading, and suchlike. In consequence everything has basically been distorted by impossible, untrue ideas. Naturally we can't therefore suddenly gain a real idea of ground rent. But we should think of ground rent simply as the economic value of the land itself in any region in relation to its productivity. Now there is a necessary relationship between this ground rent and what I stated before about a person's minimum livelihood. As you know, there are various social reformers and social revolutionaries nowadays who dream of the abolition of ground rent altogether—who believe, for instance, that ground rent will be abolished if ownership of all land is seized by the state or by society. But simply giving something a different form does not abolish it. Whether the whole municipality owns the land and estate or whether it is owned by a certain number of people does not affect that fact that a ground rent exists. It only masks the fact, assuming different forms. Defined as I defined it earlier, ground rent always exists. If you look at the ground rent for a particular region, you divide it by the number of its inhabitants and arrive at a quotient, which in turn gives rise to the only possible minimum livelihood. This is an immutable law, something like, say, the Boyle-Mariotte law in physics. And it is a primary reality, a fundamental fact, that no one really should earn more in any social organism than the sum of the whole ground rent divided by the number of inhabitants. Anything earned over and above this is earned by cooperatives and associations,[17] thus creating conditions whereby greater values accrue to one person than to another. But in reality, an individual cannot come into possession of unfixed assets worth more than I just described. And this minimum, which exists everywhere in reality, even if actual conditions hide this fact, gives rise to all economic life in so far as this economic life relates to one's unfixed assets as an individual. We have to start from this fundamental fact. That is the important thing: to start from a primary and not a secondary level. You can compare this primary fact with any other of a primary nature—say with the basic fact applicable to economic life, that any particular region has a certain quantity of raw materials. Of course you might wish this region to have more in the way of this raw product; you could work out the increased benefit you would have from the region if this were so. But you can't increase its raw resources, and that is a primary reality. It is likewise a primary fact that in reality no one in a social organism earns more—you see, you don't *earn through labour*, however much you work—than this quotient I cited. Everything over and above that amount is effected amongst people by associations and so forth.

Now political institutions can act counter to such a reality, can violate it. Therefore what needs to happen is that our thinking should come to accord with realities. That is the vital thing. Happiness amongst humankind can only arise through insight into these things. If we bring our organizing, reality-creating thinking into line with tendencies required by the very nature of the social organism, then everything else follows by itself; and then no one can feel at a disadvantage compared to another. This is a law that underlies the actual life and reality of the social organism. And you can only think about such things in the right way, only gain concepts that have a purchase on reality—I gave you the example of the relation between minimum livelihood and the ground rent—if you base them on threefolding as the founding principle. You see, only by the influence of this threefolding will people become able to shape human community so that, in any particular region, it develops in the most productive way. Life will develop most productively if it tends towards lawfulness and accords with it, rather than acting counter to it. So the important thing is to live in tune with the nature of the social organism.

But now we must clarify the following. You will not derive insight into the fundamental nature of threefolding from an external observation of life, just as little as you could derive the Theorem of Pythagoras by simply looking at right-angled triangles, however many of them you looked at. But once you have this law it can be applied universally to all right-angled triangles. This is the nature of fundamental laws: they are universally applicable once you have grasped them in the right way, in their actual relationship to reality. And you, my dear friends, also have an opportunity to grasp the need for this threefolding out of the foundations of spiritual science. Similarly, you can understand that this threefolding encompasses firstly what I will call the life of earthly spirituality: art, science, religion and, as I have said, private and criminal law too—that is one sphere. The second sphere is the political society and community of human beings, and applies to the relationship between one person and another. The third sphere is economic life, governing the relationship between the human being and what is, in a sense, inhuman, what we need so that we can raise ourselves to our true humanity. These three spheres are meant when we speak of threefolding, and in accordance with which we must seek to be members of the social organism. This is how we must engage in the social organism, for all three spheres originate in a quite different aspect of human nature itself.

All earthly life of spirit and culture is in a sense the echo—and what I say here applies to our epoch—of what we have experienced in the life before we descended to birth, to physical existence. Then we lived as a human spiritual individuality in a spiritual connection with the higher hierarchies, in spiritual connection with the disembodied souls living at present in the world of spirit and not at that moment embodied on earth. The cultural and spiritual life we develop here on earth—whether this be through religious activity or practice, in religious community; or through artistic activity; or through acting as a judge, giving a verdict on someone who has in some way violated the law or done an injustice to another person—all originates from powers which we acquired in community existence in the world of spirit before we descended into physical existence through birth. Here you must distinguish between community with other human beings in accordance with individual destiny, and community with others as I just characterized it. In earthly existence we form individual relationships with people, dependent on our individual karma, and these either draw from past lives on earth or point toward future lives. These individual, interpersonal relationships must be distinguished from others: those into which you enter by belonging, say, to a particular religious community. Here you will feel an identity in common with a number of others within this community. Or let us imagine that a book is published. Those who read it, and absorb the same thoughts from it, also form a community. Earthly cultural life, whether it relates to education or other fields, involves forming relationships with others, forming communities so that we advance spiritually through them. And all this is the expression of relationships we had in a quite different form before we descended into earthly culture. It has nothing to do with individual karma, but with what was prepared in the period we experienced in the world of spirit between death and rebirth. And so we must seek the source and origin of what I have specifically called the spiritual sphere in the life we underwent before embarking on our descent into physical existence at birth.

And then there is something we undergo and experience simply by living here on earth from birth to death. We only gradually grow into this life. Entering physical existence at birth, we still bear round us the eggshells of the world of spirit—though 'shells' is wrong, since it suggests something much harder than I mean. The child is very spiritual despite the fact that his major task is to develop the physical body. But he has much spirituality in his aura, and what he brings with him has a great affinity with the nature of earthly spiritual and cultural life. But gradually we enter more and more into the life that belongs only to the time between birth and death. In this life here, which as such bears no relation to anything in the realm of spirit, lie the sources of the life of the political state. The political state is only connected with what we undergo and experience between birth and death. And therefore only what concerns the relationship between one person and another, as people living in this life on earth, should mingle with the political life of the state. If anything else gets mixed up with this—if, for instance the state spreads its pinions over cultural or spiritual life, over Church and education, over anything other than the public life of rights between birth and death—we can say that the Prince of this World holds sway where he should not. Anything governed by state organization should be informed only by what relates to this life between birth and death.

The third sphere is the one I described as 'economic'. This economic life, which we are obliged to conduct as people who have to eat and drink, who have to dress ourselves in clothes, and so on, compels us to delve down into the sub-human realm. This chains us to something intrinsically lower than the level of our full humanity.

Having to preoccupy ourselves with economic life, we manifest something which, from a social perspective, contains more within it than we usually think. Engaged with and participating in economic life, we cannot live according to the spirit, or even according to law and justice, but we have to submerge ourselves in something sub-human. Yet precisely by so doing, something develops within us that can only develop in this way. As we organize our economic life, as we participate actively in economic life, and higher thoughts fall silent, and even interpersonal relationships only play in from their different sphere, something works itself out in our subconscious which we then bear with us into the world of spirit after passing through the gate of death. Whereas, in the life of culture and spirit on earth, we express the echo of what we experienced spiritually before we descended to earth, and whereas, in the life of rights in the political domain, we only express what belongs to the time between birth and death, when we participate in economic life, into which we cannot bring down our higher being, something prepares itself in us which is also spiritual, and which we bear with us through the portal of death. However much people might like economic life to be an earthly matter alone, it is not; but precisely because we submerge ourselves in economic life, something is prepared for us as human beings which in turn has a relationship with the supersensible world. And therefore no one should regard the organizing of economic life as being of small importance. This outward, material life, precisely, has a certain relationship with the life after death, however strange and paradoxical this may sound.

And so for those who have insight into human nature, the three spheres diverge: the purely spiritual sphere points back to pre-birth life; the sphere of politics and the state points to life between birth and death; and economic life points forward to life after death. It is truly not for nothing that we develop fraternity in economic life. In all fraternity that develops on the foundation of economic life lie the antecedents, the preconditions, for the life we develop after death. I am only giving you a brief outline here—and later we will look into these thing in greater depth—of how the threefold membering of human nature sheds light in this respect, precisely for the spiritual scientist, on how the life of society necessarily divides into three different spheres.

That is the distinctive thing about spiritual science: if we engage fully with it, it leads to directly practical outcomes. It illumines the life around us, and today people can illumine the real circumstances and conditions of life only if they engage in some way or other with spiritual science. And so it would be desirable if those who interest themselves in the spiritual-science movement would disseminate understanding to the others. You see, it is easier, relatively speaking, for the spiritual scientist to understand these matters. He knows of such things as life both before and after death from the perspective of spiritual science, and he can recognize the need for threefolding from this perspective. It is possible in our day already to recognize the need for threefolding. But a more thorough and comprehensive insight into this is gained when we also have the spiritual-scientific foundations which I have now been speaking of.

In recent centuries, you see, much pie-in-the-sky has been spoken about general morality and suchlike, sundered from external daily life by the greatest conceivable gulf. We are now in an era when we must form concepts capable of descending into daily life, that go beyond vague promises of redemption and the need to love one another. People don't love one another because they ought to. The ideas we form in these domains have to have the impetus and traction to really illumine an economic life that has grown so complex. The need for threefolding of the healthy social organism is given simply through insight into human nature.

As many people as possible should recognize this to be the primary, underlying foundation for renewal. Mere talk of the spirit, which I spoke of yesterday, may even be more harmful today than the materialism that started in the mid-nineteenth century and has gone on spreading to this day. Merely talking of the spirit, you see, merely yearning for it or invoking it, is no longer fitting for our time. What is needed in our time is to *realize* the spirit, to give it the possibility of living amongst us. It is not sufficient nowadays for people to believe in Christ. We have to realize the Christ in our actions, our work, our conduct. That is the important thing. If people can develop healthy thinking and feeling in this realm and in this respect, their thinking and feeling will also flow into something else.

Please never forget the following. A great majority of the officiating representatives of one or another Christian confession speak of Christ. I have mentioned this here in the past from other perspectives,[18] and it is important to keep illumining these things from a range of different standpoints. People speak of Christ; but if you ask them why the Christ they speak of warrants this name, they can only offer an apparent answer, and in fact are caught up in an inner lie. A great number of modern theologians speak of Christ but, since the Gospels have gradually more or less been mauled to pieces by supposed researchers, they would be unable to reply if you asked them how the Christ being as they conceive him differs from the Yahweh God, from God as such, who indwells the world as its inner essence. The great theologian Harnack[19] in Berlin wrote a book on *The Nature of Christianity*, but his account of the being of Christ is identical with the Yahweh of the Old Testament, and has precisely the same attributes. It is an inner lie to address Yahweh as Christ. And the same is true of hundreds upon hundreds, of thousands of those who preach Christianity today—for they only preach God in general, the God of whom one can say 'Ex deo nascimur'. We only find the Christ when we have experienced a kind of inner rebirth. The God we refer to when we say 'Ex deo nascimur' concerns our whole, ordinary healthy human constitution. Being an atheist actually means being ill. But we can only speak of Christ if we have experienced a kind of rebirth of the life within, of soul, something that is not simply innate in us by virtue of birth; when we experience a rebirth in our soul that accords with our current cycle of evolution.

And we can do so if we recognize that today a person is inevitably burdened with preconceptions from birth. They are innate in us, and constitute our being today. And if we stay as we were born, we bear these prejudices with us throughout life. We live in a one-sided way.

We can only redeem ourselves today through inner tolerance, by being able to engage with the opinions—even if we think them mistaken—of other people. If we have understanding, inmost understanding, for the views of other souls, even if we think they are mistaken, and if we can lovingly absorb what the other thinks and feels in the same way as what we ourselves feel and think, we acquire this capacity, this inner tolerance, and then we gradually get beyond the preconceptions and prejudices innate in us at this stage of evolution. Then we learn to say this: What you have understood in the least of my brothers, you have understood of me—for the Christ spoke to people not only at the time when Christianity began but made true his saying that 'I am with you always, even unto the end of the world.'[20] And indeed, he does keep revealing himself. It was not only once that he said, 'Inasmuch as ye have done it to the least of these my brethren, ye have done it unto me.'[21] He still says this today. He tells us that 'What you understand with inner tolerance in one of the least of my brethren, even if it is mistaken, you have understood of me, and I will enable you to overcome your prejudices if you shed them by absorbing with tolerance what the other thinks and feels.' That is one thing. In respect of thinking this is the way to come to Christ, so that Christ enters us and we not only have thoughts or ideas about him but that he lives in our thoughts. He will only do so by the means I have just described.

The second thing relates to the will. In youth we may often be idealistic, have an innate idealism. We have this simply by virtue of being born as human beings. This human idealism is no longer enough in our present evolutionary cycle. Today we need another idealism, one we educate ourselves to acquire over and above our natural human endowment, one we discipline ourselves to develop. We need an idealism we ourselves have acquired. And this is an idealism that does not fade with youth but keeps us young and idealistic throughout life. If we acquire this kind of idealism, then, founded on a non-logical yet reality-attuned law, it gives us the impetus to act not just as egoistic people but to integrate ourselves with the social organism, and to act within it. Unless we undertake, or educate ourselves, to acquire a self-cultivated idealism, we will never gain real social understanding.

We gain the 'Ex deo nascimur' by virtue of being born. The path to Christ passes on the one hand through supersensible thoughts, and on the other through the will. The path of thought involves a recognition that we are born today with prejudices and preconceptions and must shed these by tolerant engagement with the opinions of others. The path of will involves recognition that this will can only be kindled socially in the right way if we develop self-acquired idealism, an idealism that we have inculcated in ourselves through our own activity. Through this we are reborn. And what we discover in this way by acquiring it for ourselves as human beings leads alone to Christ. We cannot refer to the God of whom we say 'Ex deo nascimur' as Christ, for this is an inner untruth, a God who can also figure in the Old Testament. The God who speaks to us if we transform ourselves during our life in the two ways I have indicated, will be felt as one clearly different in nature from the Father God as such. And that is Christ. Modern theology speaks very little of *this* Christ. This Christ must enter humanity as a social impulse, whereas many today speak of Christ in a way that is nothing but an inner lie.

Things such as these cannot dawn on our understanding through merely logical reasoning. Not long ago I said to you that there is an understanding of reality which is different from merely outward, logical understanding. But when we develop in ourselves what I here described as rebirth, our thinking comes close to Christ and we learn to think and feel as we must if we are to integrate ourselves into human society today in a way that serves humanity's salvation. And then also we learn to think and feel about other matters too in the right way if we first think rightly about this fundamental thing. Cultural life today has lapsed a long way from this, and the reason is often that the modern political state has overshadowed and infiltrated it. The life of spirit and culture must be emancipated from the life of the political state in order to become fruitful again and give real impetus to human evolution. If not, all thoughts will become distorted, and distorted realities will be created as a result.

I once spoke about Wilson's definition of freedom.[22] Of course, how a modern statesman defines freedom does not have much relation to philosophical discourse. But what lives in someone when he articulates this or that idea of freedom is significant as a symptom. Wilson says we call something free that adapts itself to certain conditions so that it can move freely within them. Thus in a machine, if a basket can move freely along a conveyor belt without being impeded, we can say that the basket moves freely. Or a ship, constructed so that it runs with the wind, moves freely forward. If it were to sail against the wind, it would accordingly be unfree. And in this sense, says Wilson, a human being is likewise free if he is adapted to conditions within the social mechanism.

Less important than the fact such thoughts live in someone's head and are realized is that what is realized expresses itself in such thoughts. We can discern here whether it is healthy or runs counter to health. The idea is a total distortion. And why? You need only draw on the feelings you can gain from spiritual science when reflecting on the following. If you have adapted—and you can be very well adapted to outward circumstances, so that your life runs in accord with them and you never meet an obstacle—you are free, in this view, like a ship that sails with the wind. But this is not how we stand in the world. If the ship sails with the wind it is supposedly free—and yet at some point it has to be able to stop. It is of great importance that we can sometimes change direction, turn about, and sail against the wind so that we are not only adapted to outer conditions but can also adapt to our own inner impulses. It is hard to think of a more foolish and inept definition of freedom than Wilson's, for it contradicts human nature itself. It states the very opposite of what underlies the real nature of human freedom. If we are going to compare the human being with a ship that sails 'freely' with the wind, then we must add that it must also be able to turn around when it needs to, and sail against the wind, so that it is not compelled to be driven ever onwards. If a person must always be driven on by outer circumstances he is free only in adhering to these circumstances, but not free for his own purposes. In their modern outlook people have lost sight entirely of the human being as such:[23] there is nothing left to build on there. The human being has got lost from this modern outlook, and needs to be reintegrated into the world.

What I have now said has very, very serious aspects. I have outlined it only as a general symptom, but it has grave aspects. The human being's participation in the social organism today can be described as the ship sailing only with the wind. The capitalist system has, in particular, forced the working classes to sail with the wind only, never allowing them to stop, turn about, and sail against it to gain some peace and respite. At the public lecture in Basel[24] I said that in the capitalist economic order, the capitalist only needs the labour of the worker. In the healthy social organism, on the other hand, the capitalist also requires the respite of the labourer, requires him to need a break. The abstract capital of the capitalist system only needs labour, whereas the capital that is fed back into a purely human momentum will also require the peace and respite of the worker; will require all people to recuperate. This capital must be socially integrated into the social organism in an awareness of how the worker is both sustained by and sustains the social organism.

If we think in a healthy way within the spiritual sphere, we know perfectly well what a single, individual life is: a matter for itself, not for the social organism. But in so far as we have a life in the community, in society, we draw what we are spiritually from human community and must give it back again—and will experience the need to give it back again.

This is vital: that we equally need a worker who is spared from his labours so as to participate in spiritual, cultural life; that we have the will to give the worker respite, to spare him from his labours sufficiently to enable him also to participate in the life of spirit. That is the important thing. The gentrified economic order gradually created a gulf as I suggested yesterday; it created a cultural domain that relates only to this gentrified order and has no connection whatsoever with proletarian life. And additionally we can say that capitalism ended up requiring only the labour of the workers and not their rest.

Today such things still seem abstract, but they must no longer be so. The wholesome development of our human present and future depends on a proper understanding of these things.

Now I made a few suggestions today about a connection between various fundamental spiritual-scientific principles and the life of society. It would be so good if a spiritual movement like ours also became a small, sound and healthy social organism by acting as a vehicle for practical, living ideas informed by spiritual science. It would be an excellent thing if the gulf sundering economic, material life from spiritual life—this terrible, unhealthy division that has developed and does such harm to humanity—should finally cease. The social organism must structure itself so that a situation can no longer occur where people save up their coupons on the one hand, and in doing so are nothing more than slave-owners—since the coupons they cut out depend on a number of people unconnected to them undertaking hard labour. Then they go to Church and pray to God to save them, or attend meetings where idealistic theories of all kinds are expounded with no recognition of what nonsense it is to lead a life of spirit in the abstract, or have a connection with God while at the same time participating in slave ownership by cutting out these coupons—which is tantamount to worker exploitation. If you do not take care to make healthy distinctions, you end up sundering things in an unhealthy way. This is what has been missed and must be remedied: this abstract separation, this creating of a gulf between a cloud-cuckoo religiosity and ethics, and a daily life that is simply perpetuated with the structure that the unhealthy social organism has assumed. We have to learn to perceive these things accurately, above all seeing that the misfortunes of today spring from the gentrified distinction between the abstract and the concrete. A beginning can be made here precisely in a movement such as ours by creating a kind of small, healthy social organism, by endeavouring to get rid of everything unhealthy that may develop in such a movement, anything schismatic. The worst thing about this anthroposophically oriented spiritual movement has been the continually recurring tendencies here and there to become schismatic, to form closed groups and cliques. Without people even noticing, they strive for sectarianism of some kind. Anthroposophically oriented spiritual science must be the very opposite of this. Then it will also meet the unconscious and subconscious needs of our time, which are definitely not about forming new sects but nurturing what develops from the whole human being for all human beings, and from all human beings for the whole human being.

You can start by reflecting, my dear friends, on how to get beyond the inner factionalism within your own souls. Today sectarianism lives in us atavistically, a kind of unhealthy legacy in numerous souls. And this factionalism arises from the reluctance to carry a true life of spirit into the outward conditions of life. The same cloud-cuckoo factionalism gives rise to the objection to the appeal of which I spoke yesterday, and which I read out to you, that it is not sufficiently 'spiritual', and that it was expected of us, of all people, that it would be so. But I have never been able to speak in the expected 'spiritual' terms to such spiritual enthusiasts. When the Adler-Unold Ethical Culture Movement for moral renewal[25] began in the 1890s in America, and spread from there, I opposed it completely, since it sought to found a movement for ethics in culture based on nothing real at all, and connected with nothing in actual life—except to promulgate ethical principles. Understanding of life gained by drawing on the very foundations of life is what modern humanity needs, not phrase-mongering, not 'oughtism' about how things should be done. And in relation to the social organism, threefolding is the fundamental thing we need to reflect on, research, ponder, incorporate into people's sensibilities so that they become as well-versed in it as the two times table.

Lecture 3

DORNACH, 21 FEBRUARY 1919

It will be apparent to you that what I have presented here and on other occasions in relation to the social problems of today flows very much from spiritual-scientific foundations, and that I tried, in the appeal I spoke to you about the other day, to encompass practical ideas that inevitably emerge from deeper insight into the current state of the world. We should never tire of recollecting the thing of chief importance; and this is that ways and means must be found to enlighten people, to find opportunities to elicit understanding for the actions and deeds that humanity must embark on when we rightly grasp the nature of the social organism. You have understood, I know, that human thinking, feeling, and will also, have changed radically since the mid-fifteenth century, and that we have to entirely revise our view of history if the radical metamorphosis of mankind's state of soul in the fifth post-Atlantean epoch[26] is to be seen and understood in fruitful ways. We must recognize that the distinctive nature of evolution in this fifth post-Atlantean epoch has led to particular forms of human thinking, and equipped them with a certain type of will—whether we regard this will itself as good or bad, or right or wrong. Our whole social movement today is largely shaped by this underlying thinking and the particular forms it assumes; it is founded on the thoughts human beings can now have, which accord with the basic character of our age.

You will remember that in the threefolding of society of which we have often spoken, and which also comes to expression in the appeal I brought to your attention, the political state as such—which most people nowadays believe constitutes the entire social organism, or which at any rate they confuse with the latter—is only one sector, one limb of the threefold social organism. If you rightly understand on the one hand what the whole threefold social organism involves, and on the other try to understand how, in modern life, the social organism has become narrowly centralized, so that in a sense the state swallows it all up, then by connecting these two things you make an important contribution to understanding these matters. It is of the utmost necessity for people today that they gain serious understanding of the modern social movement. As far as necessary steps are concerned, or actions that are required, people will long continue to tap around in the dark. That is inevitable. But the thing to remember, the thing to aspire to, is to develop social insight, the possibility of really *understanding* the social organism. From this perspective it is extremely interesting to observe the actual nature of the thinking of those today who direct their social will in a particular direction. You see, we must be far less concerned with the content of their thinking than with its mode, form and configuration. As we have stressed on numerous occasions, it matters far less *what* people think than *how* they do, the orientation of their thinking. Ultimately the incisive and comprehensive nature of the contemporary world movement depends far less on whether someone is 'reactionary' in the literal sense, whether he is liberal, democratic, socialist or Bolshevist. What people say, the views they hold, are not especially important. What is vitally important is how people think, what the nature and mode of their thinking is. It is possible to find people today with radically socialist ideas, who propound a radical socialist programme—and yet the way they actually think is identical really with those who have been toppled from power the world over.

So we have to try to look at the deeper currents that are emerging. The political programmes which, as I said recently in Basel, turn up all the time as mummified views, will make very, very little difference in our changing times. What will make a difference, by contrast, is for people to learn to think differently, to shape their thoughts in a different way. Currently there is as yet nothing apart from spiritual-scientific thinking that is really guiding human thought in a new direction, and this is why most people regard it as fantasy. In fact it is the very people who accuse us of fantasy who are themselves fantasists, albeit materialistic ones. They are theoretical fantasists and cannot engage with reality. But what is taking shape now will evolve from the nature and mode of thinking. And today I'd like to consider with you something specifically related to this.

If you look at the way in which views have formed within the proletarian movement and have taken shape to this day, you find all sorts of views. Today we will focus on the fact that alongside the many other socialist workers who think in this way or that, the greatest number show a radical loyalty to Marxism, whether in its original or subsequently developed form. The notable thing here is that Karl Marx,[27] having first taken up Hegel's dialectical outlook, and acquainting himself with French social positivism, drew on these ideas in his London studies of society, of social evolution, and from this starting point formed his extraordinarily incisive socialist views, his theories, which gradually took hold of the whole proletariat. In other words, it was the Marxist *idea* that spread and, kindled by the catastrophe of the last few years, developed to the degree it has now assumed, and will continue to grow and develop. There are a large number of people amongst socialists themselves who simply call themselves Marxists. They all look back to Marx even if some remain orthodox Marxists while others represent a more progressive form of Marxism and so forth.

Now Karl Marx said something that gives us deep insight into certain aspects of these matters. Speaking of Marxism, he once said that he himself was no Marxist! My dear friends, we ought not to lose sight of this, especially in the present times. The important thing is not what is uttered or expressed but how thoughts are formed. The comfortable fashion of establishing programmes will get us nowhere in our present hardships. We can trace a path, albeit a long one, from Karl Marx himself to Vladimir Lenin,[28] who regarded himself as a genuine Marxist. And in speaking of Lenin today, we are of course not speaking just of a single individual but of a movement which one can, if one likes, subject to a thoroughgoing critique. Nevertheless it is making waves that spread far and wide, and adopting certain methods which its proponents are convinced represent authentic Marxism.

The best way to address the problem I am highlighting here is to focus on the one-sided way in which people are trying in a sense to offload everything onto the state rather than acknowledge the threefold nature of the social organism. It is certainly interesting to examine the forms of thought in Karl Marx himself: less the content of his ideas than the thought forms. If you pick up works by Marx with the notion that reading them will give you a sense of how the social organism might be shaped, you will be sorely mistaken. You will search in vain in the works of Marx for remarks about the social organism itself such as those you can find in spiritual-scientific communications that I have made here and elsewhere on the subject. This does not figure anywhere in the configurations of his thinking. In studying the economic views of society that Karl Marx himself has formulated, you will find that he simply adopts ideas about the social organism that already exist. Marx does not express original ideas about how the world ought to be. What he does do is trace how human beings thought as they introduced the modern capitalist era, and how, under its dominance, the question of wages, capital, ground rent and so forth developed. And he analyses the capitalist economy. Basically, you can find the most important ideas that Karl Marx gave the proletariat in the works of Ricardo already,[29] and others. What does Karl Marx do? He says that in the capitalist economic order as it developed in modern times, people had views that gradually gave rise to modern wage relationships, capital relationships, ground rent relationships and so on. And now he tries to think this through further. He does not say what ought to replace the social configuration that developed under capitalism but only that it inevitably led to the creation of a distinct class of human beings, the proletariat. This now exists as a reality. And now he shows where the dominance of capitalism leads—to absurd extremes so that, as it reaches its culmination it must inevitably turn into its opposite. Capital increasingly accumulates in the hands of individuals until it passes to the greatest 'individualist', which is at the same time the community or commonality of all. However Marx and the Marxists refuse to acknowledge it, they look to the state, to the civic order, as the sole and single overarching capitalist, a conglomeration that embodies all participants in the state.

Now the most varied socialist views have developed in modern times from this analysis. Karl Marx and his friend Engels[30] spent decades working to modify, expand and delimit the ideas they originally formulated, as is inevitable for someone who does not stand still but develops and keeps observing reality. Because the ideas of Marx spoke profoundly to the proletariat, as I have repeatedly shown, a great movement arose which assumed different forms in different countries. It is certainly true to say that the socialism that developed on Marxist foundations has a different nuance in England or France, and found its most radical form in Germany, passing from there to Russia. It is completely right that it took on different shades in diverse places. And yet an essential question of principle, that of the relationship of the proletarian world to the state, faded into a kind of nebulous mist. In direct consequence of this, many partisan groups formed, all opposing and bitterly contesting one another because of their different views of the relationship between the proletariat and the state as this has evolved historically in modern times. This gave rise to many different movements which we will not study in detail now. But instead let us briefly consider the path leading from Karl Marx to Lenin, since Lenin asserted he was the most authentic Marxist and understood Marx better than anyone else, whereas he thought other socialists—who also call themselves Marxists—to be renegade betrayers of the cause, and excoriated them in diverse terms, for instance as 'social chauvinists', because of their conduct during the Great War.

If we look back again to Karl Marx, as we saw, it is his thought forms that can interest us, and you can already gather something important in this respect from what I said: he formulates no positive idea of how things should develop, but his thinking has, rather, a certain dissolving tendency. Karl Marx simply states that capitalist thinkers said and did this or that, and their downfall must inevitably ensue, after which the proletariat will be in the ascendency. He does not know, nor do others, what the proletariat will do then—it will 'become apparent'. The only certain thing, he says, is that you capitalists are preparing your own downfall through measures you yourself have taken, and through what you have made of the world. But he does not know, nor do others, what the proletariat will do when it becomes dominant. This is something that will become clear eventually.

If you consider what I have just described, you can discern the form of thinking underlying it. What already exists in the world around us is simply adopted as it is and thought through. But reaching the conclusion of this thinking, the thought annihilates itself and arrives at nothing, runs as it were into the void. This is something very striking for anyone who has a sense for such things. If you study Karl Marx, you always find that you start from certain thoughts which are not in fact his, but those of the modern era. And then you find yourself propelled into something that actually disperses the ideas, confuses them, and lets them culminate in a destructive element upon which nothing can be founded.

It is extremely interesting how, in Lenin, this thought form initiated by Marx reaches its highest potency and intensification, to an almost brilliant degree. Lenin interprets Marx as an absolute opponent of the state, seeing him as building on the idea that, if the oppression of the proletariat is to end, the state, as it developed historically, must be eradicated, must cease. This is interesting because those whom Lenin saw as opponents really want to offload everything onto the state as it developed historically. In socialist circles, therefore, we have these opposites: on the one hand fanatical advocates of the state, who want the state to take over everything, and on the other, Lenin, the absolute opponent of the state. He sees the redemption of humanity not in the abolition of the state, which he regards as nonsense, but in its gradual withering. And if we study his thinking here, we come to the thought-form that lives in him. This is interesting.

Lenin thinks as follows: the proletariat is the only class which, after the others have reached absurd extremes, is ready and able to become dominant. This proletarian class, thinks Lenin, will drive the former bourgeoisie-governed state to its highest perfection. Attend here to the form of his thinking. So Lenin does not say, like the anarchists, 'Let's abolish the state'. No, this does not even occur to him. He is an opponent of anarchism. He thinks that abolishing the state is complete idiocy. Instead he says that if things go on developing in the way initiated by the bourgeoisie, the latter will be ripe for downfall. The proletariat will take possession of what he calls the 'machinery of the state'. The state founded by the bourgeoisie as a tool to oppress the proletariat will be perfected by the latter, and therefore they will create the most perfect state. But what is the character of this perfected state? Lenin now asks. And he thinks himself a genuine Marxist when he says that, if this perfect state develops—which it will through the proletariat, arising as the ultimate consequence of the bourgeois class—it will be distinguished by the fact that it withers away. The state as it is at present can only exist as a state created by the bourgeoisie; and when the proletariat develops it fully, leads what the bourgeoisie began to its final culmination, this state will acquire its true momentum which consists in ceasing by itself.

This is the characteristic form of Lenin's thinking. We find here an intensification of what was already present in Marx: the thought that is developed and then fades into nothing. Except that Lenin is a very realistic thinker who, drawing on historical precedents, arrives at the idea that the state must be perfected. That it does not die at present is because it is imperfect, for this is what gives it its life force. When the proletariat perfects it, he thinks, this provides the basis for its gradual withering.

You see, an idea is drawn from reality, and this idea today has the tendency in large parts of eastern Europe to unfold again into reality.

It is not a mere idea; it passes into reality. It leads to the following assertions: that you bourgeois classes gave rise to this modern state, and used it only as a tool to suppress the proletariat. You left it imperfect, as the state of the advantaged classes. It serves as your means of oppressing the proletarian class, and it owes its life and viability to this. Now the proletariat will rise up and abolish the rule of the bourgeoisie and make the state perfect—at which point it will die, will be unable to live. And then whatever should develop will develop, and no one, as Lenin says, can predict what this will be in advance. This socialism gives rise therefore to unknowing. And this is very interesting, for the mode of thinking that has taken hold of sociological ideas today is drawn from science; and just as science rightly formulates its unknowingness, so socialist thinking similarly arrives at its 'Ignorabimus'—'we do not know and will not know'.[31]

My dear friends, it is important to gain insight into this connection. Socialism would not exist without everything taught by those of a scientific outlook at all, the 'bourgeois', middle-class universities. Socialism is a child of the bourgeoisie. Even Bolshevism is a child of the bourgeoisie. This is the deeper connection and context, and one it is vital that we recognize.

Once we have understood the nature of this form of thinking we can draw important conclusions about the outlook of a man such as Lenin. For instance, he lays special emphasis on the development of bureaucracy within the bourgeois state, what he calls its 'military machinery'. This bureaucratic, military machinery arose because the ruling classes need it to suppress the oppressed classes. And this is why the most radical wing of socialism, Bolshevism, propounds the view that what it desires can only be realized by an armed proletariat, by armed struggle. Without weapons, what this side wants has no prospect of success, and this is illustrated by historical instances. The French communes could only hold sway while their leaders possessed weapons. The moment they were disarmed, it was over for them. This is one of the points to recognize—the view of the proletariat as armed workers. And what is to be achieved by this armed proletariat? Well, this is already happening today to some extent, happening in a way that makes it seem as if some people might perhaps awaken from the deep social slumber in which they have been so long wrapped. What is the intention? Above all, the class-bound state is meant to end. Armed workers are to seize hold of the class state founded by the bourgeoisie.

And now it is interesting to find that those, particularly, who have developed the thought-form of modern socialist thinking to a rather brilliant degree, give clear and palpable expression to what has become rooted in proletarian souls through circumstances, through historical developments. Lenin, for example, states that the hierarchy of the military and the bureaucrats should be replaced by a kind of administration consisting, however, only of elected members; and he points out that, as circumstances are today, one requires no background or experience for administering whatever needs to be administered other than ordinary general schooling. He himself uses a curious formulation which tells us a great deal. Lenin says that what is called the 'state' nowadays should be transformed so that it becomes, really, a great factory with common accounts. To achieve this, and to maintain checks and balances and so on, it will be enough to master the four processes in arithmetic, as taught in every school.

My dear friends, we ought not merely to ridicule such things, but recognize that this view is in fact nothing other than the ultimate consequence of middle-class outlooks. Just as our modern social forms first arose as purely economic entities, so we must say that those with capital assets, those in control of capital, mostly have nothing more in their heads than Lenin requires of the worker supervisors of the future.

If it had been possible for the proletarian class, as it has emerged in recent times, to look up to figures in whose special capacities or suchlike they could believe, to whom they could look up as to a certain justified authority, then everything would have taken a different course. But there is no one to look up to. They can only look to those who, basically, have the same mental qualities as they do, and are otherwise distinguished only by virtue of their wealth. There is no intrinsic difference between them and those who govern them. In Lenin we simply find this expressed in strict, theoretical formulations.

In Lenin's radical formulations we can therefore grasp how things arose. Now of course the following question will be on the tip of your tongues: yes, but so many dire things emerge from this, it is all so terrible. And yet, nevertheless, we must look things squarely in the face and, however uncomfortable, engage with the way people think. Of course, if the results of socialism are described, we can easily feel middle-class outrage, which leads more often than not to middle-class angst as well. But the urge to really understand things is not particularly apparent in our day.

Now to understand what is already occurring and especially what is still going to, it is essential to consider the following. Lenin, who regards himself as a genuine Marxist, points out that Marx introduced a particular view of the development of the social order in modern times and for the future. These people think, really, that the reshaping of society must take place in two phases, not at a single stroke. The first phase is simply that that the proletariat takes over the bourgeois form of the state, which Lenin believes will wither away by itself once it is perfected. The proletariat will take over this bourgeois state, changing it in line with the workers' views and impulses, and lead it towards its demise. Marx himself already explained that this in itself will not yet lead to any desirable conditions. What will this first phase of Marxist-Leninist socialization lead to? In banal terms—but these people themselves present it in banal terms—it will lead to circumstances in which those who do not work cannot eat either; that each person will have a particular work or labour to perform, and that in consequence of this he will have the right to items necessary for his subsistence, from, let us say, the state machinery and so forth. But adherents of these views are clear that this in itself will not lead to equality between people. Rather, it will simply perpetuate inequality. Nor will it lead to a situation where a person really possesses the yield from his work. Karl Marx emphasizes this, as does Lenin. The community—that is, the state, or whatever you like to call it, whatever remains of the bourgeois world order—must subtract from such yield whatever is needed for schooling, or to support particular enterprises and so forth. Lasalle's[32] old idea of the right to the full yield from one's work must naturally be dropped in the context of this socialism. But this does not, nevertheless, lead to any kind of equality. For you see, people as such, even if they perform the same work, have different demands on life due to their particular circumstances. Of course this socialism acknowledges this; and it immediately gives rise in turn to inequality. In summary, these socialists believe that in this first phase of the socialist order, the bourgeois order will simply be perpetuated when the proletariat takes it over.

It is very interesting how Lenin speaks directly of this, saying, for instance, in one passage of his book *The State and Revolution*,[33] that something like the bourgeois order, the bourgeois state, will arise without the bourgeoisie. So here you can see in Lenin's own words— that the bourgeois state will exist without the bourgeoisie—something I continually stress, and consider extremely important: that those who hold socialist views today are only the inheritors of the bourgeoisie, have merely taken on its mantle. The ideas are bourgeois ideas. A man such as Lenin, who takes the Marxist form of thought a brilliant stage further, says that the next phase is to have a bourgeois state without the bourgeoisie, who will either be killed off or become a serving caste. There will be no equality; you will just have the proletariat on top, with elections replacing the appointments made by monarchs or other similar ruling structures. The proletariat will govern and legislate at the same time. But it is still the bourgeois state, just without the bourgeoisie. Each person will receive a wage for his work, but this does not get rid of inequality of course.

None of this creates ideal conditions. So if someone asks, 'What have these folk made of the human social order?' then Lenin would simply reply, 'In the first phase we did not promise you anything more than to fulfil the consequences of what you founded as bourgeois state, and, as proletarians that is what we will do. Before, it was you who ran things, now we will. We will do the same as you did: a bourgeois state without the bourgeoisie.'

Lenin says, for example, that this bourgeois state without the bourgeoisie will lead to the withering of the state. The state will have died away entirely once society has implemented the rules it regards as its ideal, and when an end comes to the narrow scope of civil law in which, with the hard-heartedness of Shylock,[34] people calculate whether one person has worked half an hour longer or has received a slightly lower wage than another. This narrow scope of rights will only be superseded at the end of the first phase. Until the end of the first phase the bourgeois civil state and legislature will survive, and will even be intensified, with all its mean calculations. This bourgeois, Shylockian outlook will therefore continue through the first phase of socialism.

And here you have the only thing these people promise. They say: You created this, initially to serve the interests of your class; and now we will perpetuate it for the proletariat. It is nonsense to speak of democracy, since democracy would only lead to a suppression of the minority. The proletariat will continue to do everything as you did. But by doing so it will cause the death of what you awoke to seeming life. Only then will the second phase arrive.

Karl Marx also already pointed to this second phase of socialism, as did Lenin after him, but the latter in a very curious way. And I consider it extremely important that we recognize this. Picture this: Marx in the shape of Lenin—they will drive the bourgeois social order to its ultimate consequences, and then the state will wither away, and people will no longer be accustomed to needing the legislating state, or any state at all. The state will cease. It will gradually become entirely unnecessary to have a state, since nothing that the state undertakes will need to be done any more. The period during which everyone was paid on the principle of 'work or starve' will come to an end. That was the first phase of socialism. Then the time will come when each person will be able to live according to his capacities and needs, not according to the work he performs. And this will be the higher stage, towards achieving which everything preceding it was only a transition. No one will ask any longer whether someone has worked half an hour less, or more. And only then will the time arrive when the equal value of mental and artistic work is recognized. Through the natural social order each person will stand at his post and position, each not only working according to his capacities but wishing to do so, since, through civilized existence in the first phase people will have become accustomed to regard work not as something they are impelled to do but which they fervently desire to. And so it will come about that each person will gain his subsistence according to his needs. Instead of a mean-spirited civic and legal order in which everything is calculated down to the minute, people will recognize that a person who does a particular kind of work might work, say, two hours less, and that each person can live and work according to his capacities and needs. That is the higher social order. All transitions towards achieving it, so as to lead the bourgeois state towards its end and demise, culminate in the 'Ignorabimus'—'we do not know what will happen'—which, on the other hand however, is regarded as development of the second, higher phase of socialism.

But it is interesting what Lenin says of this higher phase of socialism. He calls it ignorance to claim that people as they are nowadays could be induced to embrace a social order where everyone can live according to his capacities and needs—ignorance. No socialist can think of promising that the higher developmental phase of communism will inevitably arrive. The prospect of such an era entertained by the great socialists presupposes a productivity of labour and a type of human being very far removed from what exists today; far removed from modern people who will take whatever they can get, and would ask for the sky if they thought they could get it. This is an extremely interesting and important comment. First phase: socialization with people as they are; then the ultimate consequence of the bourgeois world order: a state that withers away through its own qualities and characteristics, giving way to a higher phase with human beings who have grown quite different from how they are now—a new type of human being.

You see, that is the abstract ideal: to bring to its absurd, self-fulfilling end the bourgeois order and induce the state to wither away, and in this process to cultivate a new type of humanity whose members will be accustomed to working according to their capacities and therefore also living according to their needs. It will be impossible for anyone to steal because, just as when decent people object nowadays if anyone denigrates a lady, decent people—and all will be decent—will repudiate such things. There will be no need for military or bureaucratic enforcement; it will be a different kind of human being. And what faith is all this founded on my dear friends? On a superstitious faith in the economic order. Remember this. Capitalism created an economic order devoid of any counterpart in a real life of spirit, but just an ideology. And this is the condition that socialism seeks to drive to an extreme: everything must go, apart from economic activity. And yet on the other hand socialism believes that this will produce a new kind of humanity.

It is really vital to recognize this superstitious faith in economic life, to see that a huge number of people nowadays believe that if economic life were to be established as they see fit, not only would a desirable social order develop but even a whole new type of humanity, one that will accord with a desirable social order.

All this is a modern form of superstition, one that cannot recognize that, behind all outward economic and material reality, the spiritual and its impulses hold sway and must be perceived and taken up by people. This is a wholesale failure to acknowledge the spirit. If humanity is to recover, this can only be through spiritual means, only by human beings integrating spiritual impulses as spiritual cognition, and as social thinking and social feeling founded on spiritual science. Economic evolutions will never engender a new humanity. This can only happen from within; and for this to come about, the life of spirit and culture must be freely founded upon itself. A life of culture as this developed over the past few centuries, formerly bound by the cameralistic,[35] revenue-governing state and now by the economic state, will never be able really to engender this new humanity. For this reason, we must strive on the one hand for the freedom of the life of spirit by according spiritual, cultural life its own sector. And then, on the other, we must strive to conduct economic life in accordance only with its own intrinsic laws, so that the state, which only has to do with the relationship between one person and another, does not involve itself in economic affairs. You see, economic life focuses on consuming everything that enters its sphere. In so far as we stand within economic life, we are consumed, and must continually save ourselves from being swallowed up. We can do so if we establish a fitting civil relationship between every person, which falls within the sphere of the regulating activity of the state as such.

If we consider with an open mind things such as those we have considered today, we see that the impulses which have emerged in the modern social movement are filled with a thinking that really culminates in a void. Imagine if the best maxim for education were to be formulated as follows: that we educate people to absorb as much of the death principle as possible—so that, once educated, they will if possible begin to die. This would be an idea, a thought which annihilates its own reality. But if we return to Lenin's idea of the state, that once perfected it readies itself to die, we see that modern thinking is unable to form a productive, fruitful idea. It cannot do so in the realm of spirit because the life of spirit has become mere ideology here, comes to consist of mere thoughts or laws of nature, which are likewise only thoughts; and also because this life of spirit is bound, chained, by economic or political life. The catastrophic war also taught us this especially. Consider to what degree this kind of culture dictated it. Here we saw this enchainment in the most terrible form, spreading across the globe. And then you will have seen it in the political sphere: the socialists, who think the half-thoughts of bourgeois life through to their end, conceive of a state characterized by the fact that it induces its own demise. And in the sphere of economic life, all surrender to the superstition, the blind faith that this economic life, which in reality devours and consumes us—and to counter which we must have the two other sectors—will produce a new kind of humanity.

Modern thinking has not managed to arrive at anything, in any field, that can create life-sustaining conditions. And so we can say that what we seek to achieve on the foundations of spiritual science is to shape conditions worthy of life from ones fit only for death. But it cannot be a matter here of what many today hope for, and what has even already happened here or there: that those who have been on the bottom of the pile should be at the top and vice versa, the only difference being that the ones at the bottom thought in reactionary or bourgeois ways when they were cock of the roost, while those who are now on top think as socialists. The forms of thought are basically no different, since there is an important distinction between *what* someone thinks and *how* he thinks. As soon as you understand this, you have the basis for understanding this threefolding of the social organism, which engages with reality, which must unfold and emerge as the health of the social organism.

In this field we really have to recognize that the most important thing needed by our times must be drawn from spiritual-scientific cognition and perception. We must take care not to overlook this very, very serious and significant aspect of our spiritual-scientific movement. But my dear friends, we do overlook this if we allow ourselves, in particular in the context of anthroposophically oriented spiritual knowledge, to be seduced into any kind of sectarianism. Each and every one should scrutinize himself and ask how much factionalism he still harbours within. You see, the modern movement of humanity depends on eradicating everything schismatic from this movement, not being factional, not abstract, but a friend to human beings; to gain broad perspectives rather than narrow, schismatic ones. In as much as this movement of ours emerged in a sense from the theosophical movement, it contains potential seeds of sectarianism, which we must thwart. Everything factional must be eradicated. And what we need first and foremost are broad horizons, an open-minded view of reality.

Recently I said that in cutting out their savings coupons, people should realize that these contain human labour, and that in so far as human labour is slavery in the capitalist economic order, they are participating at least partly in slavery. It is no good replying, 'Oh, that's terrible!' or suchlike, for this 'Oh, that's terrible' is the worst abstraction and can easily seduce us into modern factionalism. I have often said the same thing in a different way. People hear me speak about Lucifer and Ahriman and they think, 'Oh, goodness me, let's keep them at arm's length, we want nothing to do with Lucifer or Ahriman; let us cleave to the good God.' But by such abstraction they succumb all the more to Lucifer and Ahriman. It is important to have the honesty and authenticity to know that we are embedded in the modern social process and cannot avoid it by any kind of self-deception. Instead we should do our utmost to help heal this social process in its entirety. As humanity has evolved, the individual cannot help himself as such but must play his part in helping poor humanity. It is not a matter nowadays of thinking we will be good human beings, will sit down and send out loving thoughts to all humanity and suchlike, but rather of recognizing that we are intricately involved in this social process and of developing the ability to be bad along with bad humanity—not because it is good to be bad but because a social order that must be overcome, must be developed into something different, compels us to live in this way. We ought not to want to live in illusion about how morally sound we are and pride ourselves on being better than others, but to acknowledge that we are complicit, are part of it. The less we succumb to illusions, the more we can develop collaborative momentum to bring about what leads to the healing of the social organism, to master the ability to wake up out of the state of slumber in which people today are so deeply wrapped. And nothing else will do here but the capacity to form more energetic thoughts, more incisive thoughts, as we find these in spiritual science; to counter the weak, tired, lame thoughts at present inhabiting mainstream science, official academe.

I recall that about 18 or 19 years ago, at the Berlin Workers' Association,[36] I once spoke of how modern scholarship, modern science, is a bourgeois affair, and how, as we evolve, we must try to liberate thoughts in particular, scholarship, from this bourgeois, gentrified element. But the leaders of the proletarian movement today simply do not grasp this, certain that the bourgeois thought they have adopted is an absolute good, that what is true is true. It does not occur to the socialists to consider this this 'truth' is connected with middle-class precedents. They speak of the impulses, the emotions of the proletariat, but they themselves think in entirely bourgeois, gentrified ways. Now I'm sure that many of you will object that what is true is simply true. Indeed, my dear friends; yes, certainly, a particular sum of truths about, say, chemistry or physics or mathematics is of course true. There is no such thing as a bourgeois truth being different from a proletarian truth. Certainly, the Theorem of Pythagoras cannot be true in only a bourgeois or a proletarian way and so forth. That is not what I mean. What I mean is that the truths in question encompass a certain field or sphere.

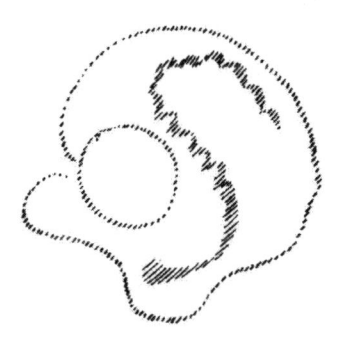

If we stay within this field, what is contained within it is of course true, but such truths are useful, comfortable and appropriate precisely for middle-class circles, and outside it [see drawing] lie various other things that can also be known but are overlooked by received opinion. It is not a matter here of the truth of truths in chemistry or mathematics, but of there being other truths beyond them which alone shed the right light on them, put them in the right context, giving them a very different complexion, thus embedding science or scholarship within a broader context that can then no longer be bourgeois. Whether things are true or not matters less than what one seeks to gain from truth. And there are subtle distinctions to be made here, even, in the quality of truth. The professors of chemistry at universities will not be able to make any particular erratic leaps in their thinking. For, a chemistry professor, an expert in his field, working in his lab, knows that he himself is thinking least of all: the methodologies are thinking for him, and so forth. But as soon as this same thinking addresses history, or the history of literature, anything that raises people from economic life and brings them into a sphere worthy of humankind, the cat is out of the bag. And history as it is at present is nothing more than a bourgeois *fable convenue*, an agreed fable. And the same applies to philosophy and other disciplines, though people have no inkling of this and take them to be objective.

Health and life can only take root here if we return academe and scholarship to their own self-administration or, in a nutshell, if we introduce the threefolding I have often referred to.

I have to make a small correction. Recently, when speaking of the forming of the German committee in Stuttgart to promote our appeal, I said that it consisted of Messrs Boos, Molt and Kühn. But I have been told that our friend Dr Unger[37] is also playing an important part, and this should not be forgotten.

Now, my dear friends, today I have been trying to shed light on things again from the contemporary angle. I am really very concerned that we seek to delve ever deeper into the social problem from the perspective of spiritual science. You have the foundations now for understanding it, and understanding is what we need first of all. As we study our modern times, as I have said previously, we will not imagine that an appeal such as this and everything resulting from it, can lead to an immediate, successful outcome. The lectures I gave in Zurich, in expanded form and with the addition of further specific issues, are about to be published in book form,[38] and so the brief, condensed contents of the appeal will be available in full detail. Before anything changes, the movements that practise ruthless exploitation will really first bring themselves to absurd extremes, will end in creating complete perplexity and dire misfortune. That is inevitable. But we must still create something at the right moment which people can later look back to and draw upon once the old has led them to absurd extremes. And that is why it is so infinitely necessary that the impulses implanted in your hearts should not be left to wither again but that you do your part, each wherever he can, to help cultivate what must necessarily come about.[39]

Lecture 4

DORNACH, 1 MARCH 1919

In the course of these reflections[40] I have drawn attention to the fact, apparent as humanity evolves, that deep within the human soul, in the unconscious interior of the human soul, something quite different can occur from what manifests at a more surface level. As we have often heard, a person can think that he is striving for a particular thing whereas in truth he bears in the depths of his soul impulses that tend in a very different direction. This is a truth of particular relevance today. Nowadays we see a whole class of human beings in the grip of a particular type of will, one we have often spoken of. And precisely here we find something developing at the soul's surface, consciousness developing in this age of the consciousness soul, which is very, very different from impulses in the soul's depths that seek realization, and of which today nothing real is as yet present in our consciousness.

If we study what lives in the consciousness of the modern proletariat, we find it to be filled with three things, as we have often mentioned. Firstly, a materialistic view of history. Secondly, the view that everything that happens in the world has always so far been founded on class warfare, that this class warfare accounts for everything that happens and that what appears to be different in nature is only a reflection of this. And thirdly, as I have often characterized it, the doctrine of 'added value'[41] which concerns the additional value accruing from workers' unpaid labour, constituting the profit the employer takes from the worker without the latter receiving any remuneration for it. Basically, proletarian consciousness is constituted of these three aspects and gives rise to the impulses from which the modern social movement draws the various views and judgements at work in it. This is what lives in the mind of the proletarian class.

But three other things live in the consciousness of modern humanity, live also in the deeper layers of soul of the proletariat and elicit their feelings especially. But the world today normally has very little awareness of these three things. The world does not seek much self-knowledge, and therefore knows nothing of what lives in the depths of the soul and strives to be realized in history. These three other things are, firstly, a penetration of spiritual life in a way appropriate for our era—what we can call spiritual science of one kind or another. The second is freedom in our life of thinking, freedom of thought. And the third is socialism in the genuine sense of the word. The proletariat, too, strive for these three things but know nothing of them. And in their instincts they pursue the other three things which, as I said, work at the surface of soul life, in their conscious mind.

There is a complete contrast, it is clear, between conscious strivings of the proletariat and their subconscious impulses. Consider the materialistic outlook, which emerged from the materialism of the modern era over the past four centuries. Amongst the ruling classes of mankind, this materialism first made itself felt in the field of science, spreading from there to all academic disciplines in general. Amongst the modern proletariat, which basically simply adopted the legacy of the scientifically-oriented, academic mode of thinking, this turned into a materialistic view of history; and this assumes that all spiritual and cultural life is really only a kind of vapour rising from the activities of economic life, from everything occurring in the domain of economic life. This outlook considers that the only realities in human life must be ascribed to the production of goods, trade, and consumption; and that, depending on the ways in which the economy was organized in a particular era, people cultivated this or that religious belief, this or that form of art, and this or that legal and ethical system. Cultural life is here seen largely as an ideology, that is, it has no intrinsic reality but is a reflection of the economic struggles and battles occurring in the world. The thoughts and ideas people formulate, their artistic feelings, whatever they express in moral intentions, can work back in turn on these economic struggles. But ultimately, it is thought, all culture is a reflection of outer, economic life. And this is more or less the materialistic view of history. But if human life is only a mirror image of merely external, material, economic forces, and if, in addition, the world is only a sensory arena, and human thoughts only reflect sensory reality, and if human beings seek only to think about and acknowledge as real what is manifest in the sense world, then they turn their back on all true life of the spirit; and this means in turn that they dispense with any idea of an independent, inwardly self-contained spirit within them.

In the modern era people have increasingly sought to offer proofs that there is no such thing as an independent spirit alive in the supersensible realm, that spirit itself does not exist. This sense of things lives at the surface of modern soul life and largely constitutes the content of modern consciousness since the advent of the era of the consciousness soul. But in the profoundest depths of soul-life, nevertheless, modern humanity is seeking for the spirit. It has what one might call a deep and inmost need for it. A glance at human evolution and human history can demonstrate this.

We have often cast our gaze back to the distinctive disposition and outlook of the early post-Atlantean period, that of early Indian culture. We characterized this era from all kinds of perspectives; and anyone who can look at things with an open mind will have learned that the spiritual way of life and thought at that ancient time—the Indian cultural period as only spiritual science can properly discern it—is founded on unconscious intuitions. Please note that I say *unconscious* intuitions, for the life of spirit and culture at the time was atavistic. In this first post-Atlantean cultural epoch, we can say, unconscious intuitions were the fount and wellspring of cultural life.

Then, as we move forward through evolution, we come to the

Ancient Persian epoch, and seeking its source we will find that this cultural and spiritual life of Ancient Persia flowed from unconscious inspirations.

The cultural life of the third epoch, that of Egypt-Chaldea, flowed from unconscious imaginations. This Egyptian-Chaldean life of culture finds its way into the earliest historical records, and if we look at history without preconceptions we can discover that unconscious imaginations living in the soul faculties of Egyptians and Chaldeans composed their ancient forms of knowledge.

Then followed the Graeco-Roman epoch. Imaginations still survived in the culture of those times, but they began now to be pervaded by concepts and ideas. A salient aspect of Greek culture was that the Greeks were the first people in human evolution to possess a new inner faculty, that of ideas and concepts. I have described this in more detail in my book *Riddles of Philosophy*.[42] Nevertheless, all the concepts of the Greeks were imbued with a pictorial quality, with imaginations. People overlook this nowadays, especially in that peculiar version of Greek culture taught in grammar schools and universities. When a Greek said the word 'idea', for instance, this was something he saw in his mind's eye, not a merely abstract concept as it has become for us today. When he uttered this word, he had the sense that something visionary hovered before him which then however was clearly formulated in a concept. It was something tangible and seen. 'Idea' is at the same time 'sight'. You couldn't have had the word 'ideology' in ancient Greece really, even though this word is taken from the Greek; or at least you couldn't have had it with the sense and meaning with which it has been endowed today, and this was because ideas were, for the ancient Greek, something imbued with image.

> I. Ancient Indian cultural epoch:
>   Unconscious intuitions as the source of culture
> II. Ancient Persian cultural epoch:
>   Unconscious inspirations as the source of cultural life
> III. Egypto-Chaldean cultural epoch:

Unconscious imaginations as the source of cultural life
IV. Graeco-Roman cultural epoch:
Unconscious imaginations with ideas
V. Modern era:
Concepts that strive towards imaginations[43]

Now the curious thing is that in our fifth post-Atlantean era, imaginations have for the time being faded and been lost, leaving the concepts of the consciousness soul. Our modern culture is so prosaic and dry, with everything pictorial squeezed out of it, leaving only the abstraction which people who aspire to be cultured and educated are especially fond of. The modern age feeds on abstractions and seeks to reduce everything, really everything, to some abstract concept or other. We find the abstract concept holding sway most comprehensively precisely in what people regard as their civic pragmatism. But in the depths of human souls something else is already stirring, and this is characteristic of the time we are in now and will be so especially in the near future: in their subconscious impulses people are turning again toward imaginations, striving toward them. So we can speak of concepts seeking to be imaginations again.

Our spiritual science addresses this search for imaginations. But the large majority of humankind is as yet unaware of these underdepths of the soul. People therefore regard culture in terms of mere concepts, mere ideas, which leave them fairly helpless. Concepts as such are devoid of content. And hitherto it has been the fate of the governing classes to develop, increasingly, a penchant for purely conceptual thinking—which in turn gave rise to something else. This purely conceptual thinking is impotent, and engenders an adherence, a dependency, on the reality that cannot be refuted because it is available to the senses: outward, sense reality. This belief in merely outward sensory reality has very largely arisen from modern humanity's conceptual impotence.

The impotence of conceptual life comes to expression in all realms of culture. In science the chief focus is on experimentation so as to allow something to emerge that does not otherwise figure in the sense world—since, if you merely reflect on the sense world you never get beyond it. Concepts themselves contain no reality.

In art, people have increasingly become accustomed to worshipping the model, still life—adhering entirely to outer objects. And it has largely been the fate of leading figures in humanity so far to aspire ever more to a kind of mere study of external, sensory reality. They endeavoured increasingly to grasp and record outward sense reality, losing sight of how to draw on the spirit and present this through the medium of art. Naturalism became the aim, an imitation of what nature presents to our outward senses, and this was because abstract culture had no fount or spring from which something autonomous could be drawn and fashioned.

If you consider the development of modern art, you will find confirmation of this everywhere. These newer arts sought naturalism as far as possible, a representation of outer perceptions of reality. In the end this culminated in what was called Impressionism. Prior to this, artists were seeking to depict outer objects; but then came those who drew the ultimate consequence of all this. It seemed to them that when looking at a human figure or a forest, and painting them, they were not actually reproducing their true impressions. How could they be true to nature, they wondered, if the sun shines on foliage in one way at one moment but then the light changes again, and creates quite different conditions? They saw that they could not precisely record what the outer world showed them since it keeps assuming a different countenance. Or, in trying to paint a smiling person, they were aware that his face might change a moment later into some quite different expression, a frown, say. Should they therefore paint the frown over the smile? If I want to depict the enduring nature of objects in time, this will constrain the objects themselves. Natural scenes cannot be constrained but human subjects can be by getting the model to sit very still and hold a single pose or expression as far as possible. But if you try to paint them like this they will easily appear rigid, frozen, if you're seeking to be naturalistic. That doesn't work. And so these artists became Impressionists, trying only to record their immediate, transient impression. But then you cannot be entirely naturalistic any more but must use all kinds of means not to imitate nature as such but to evoke the appearance, the impression which nature makes on you at any particular moment. And here lay the problem: to be absolutely naturalistic, people turned to Impressionism; and yet in Impressionism they could no longer be naturalistic! Everything was reversed. And now some tried no longer to depict impressions, no longer to record outer impressions, but to give shape to what rose up within them, however primitive this might be. They sought to hold fast to the inner response rising within them. And these artists became Expressionists instead.

We could trace the same development in the realm of moral life, and even in the life of rights: everywhere this striving that arises from a predilection for abstract culture. You just have to study recent developments in humanity in the right way and then you will discover the search for abstraction everywhere.

What became of this for the modern proletariat? When it was harnessed to the factory, to the machine, harnessed to modern, soulless capitalism, the whole destiny of the proletarians became chained to economic life. The same way of thinking that led the cultured elite to naturalism, gave the proletariat a doctrine that manifests in the materialistic view of history. Wherever one looks one sees that the proletariat merely drew the ultimate consequences of what had developed amongst the bourgeois class—consequences from which the members of this same class step back in such horror and alarm.

And what was the stance towards religion amongst these bourgeois circles? In one respect, for instance, religious attitudes remained as follows: formerly people had obscure, atavistic ideas about the Christ mystery. They had developed various ideas about how Christ dwelt within Jesus. During the nineteenth century, abstract culture meant that people could no longer picture how Christ lived within Jesus, and so they confined themselves to the sense-perceptible events that had unfolded at the beginning of the Christian era, to mere Jesuology. Jesus was increasingly seen as an outward person. The Christ who belongs to the world of spirit increasingly faded from view. Abstract soul-life found no path to Christ and made do with Jesus instead. What did proletarian consciousness make of this? In the proletarian mind it seemed that there was no particular need for any special religious view of Jesus. The middle classes had already made Jesus into the 'simple man of Nazareth'. And since the working classes saw themselves as dependent on economic life, they thought this must have been true of him too. It seemed to them that he said what he did based on the economic circumstances in which he found himself, and that no one therefore should ascribe to him any special mission outside of his simple, plain existence. They believed that one should just study the economic conditions that prevailed in Palestine when Christianity began, and would discover in the process why Jesus said what he did, why he threw down the tools of his trade and wandered around uttering all kinds of ideas. One of the ultimate consequences of modern Protestant theology is the materialistic Jesus doctrine of the modern proletariat, which no longer has any power to sustain our humanity.

As far as the second thing is concerned, freedom in thinking, inner initiative in thought, once again it is modern humanity's subconscious, deeper soul interior that seeks this. What lives at the conscious surface of the soul believes that it should strive for the very opposite, and does indeed do so. And so the subconscious rumbles in radical opposition and this conflict comes to expression in the terrible battles that rage nowadays. The modern ruling classes seek to shake off any higher authority and yet they have tipped over into all kinds of faith in authority. Above all they have fallen into a blind faith in the authority of the state, which has become the highest idol for the bourgeoisie.

Nothing seems more important to the middle classes today than a 'professional judgement'! They turn to the 'experts' at every opportunity and allow these professional verdicts to inform their outward lives. Anyone who enters public life with the rubber stamp of a university degree is apparently qualified to say what's what. If he is a theologian, he can be asked what God is planning for humanity. If he is a jurist, you can ask him about the nature of the law. If he is a physician, you can ask him about human health. And if he has emerged from any of the philosophy faculties, you can ask him absolutely anything about the world. Some at least have always smiled when any reference was made to a book by the venerable pre-Kantian philosopher Wolf,[44] the title of which is, roughly, 'On the Nature of the Human Soul, on the State, on History and on All Rational Matters in General'. People smile at the title; and yet leading circles in modern times hold firmly to the view that the whole content of reasoned discourse is to be found brewing in the mental laboratories that the state has established for human benefit. In other words, these leading circles, the ruling classes, have made no efforts whatsoever for all people to develop their own minds, but instead cultivate a uniform mentality, trying to ensure that this is, basically, a state-governed mentality. Modern consciousness has become 'state consciousness' to a far greater degree than people actually credit. They think of the state as their god, which gives them what they require. They need not concern themselves with things directly since the state will ensure that all rational aspects of life are regulated for them.

The proletariat was excluded from involvement in the life of the state excepting for a few areas where democratic structures were built into it. The working classes, with the labour that encompasses and draws upon the whole of a person's nature, were instead harnessed to economic activity. And in turn the workers drew the ultimate consequence of this for their life. The modern, middle-class citizen has a state consciousness even if he doesn't always admit this, and gladly creates more and more state with this state consciousness. Besides having your business cards printed with the appellation 'Reserve Lieutenant *and* Professor' there are many other ways of 'making state'. But the proletarians had no interest in the state. They were harnessed to economic life, and therefore their feelings became the ultimate consequence of middle-class feeling, but in a manner appropriate to their lives. Their consciousness became the class consciousness of the proletariat. And so we can see, really—since the proletariat has nothing to do with the state—that this class consciousness is founded on internationalism. These things are inevitable. The bourgeois mentality only inclined to the state because it tends to middle-class needs, and the middle classes wish to be tended. But the state doesn't look after the proletarians, and so they only feel connected to the world in so far as they belong to their class, the working class. And this proletarian class has proceeded in the same way in all countries and states. For this reason the international proletariat developed, and felt itself to be in stark and conscious opposition to all bourgeois existence, yet strove with this power of consciousness for statehood, for state-like factors. In the modern era the development of this class consciousness within the proletariat has assumed extraordinary suggestive forms. I don't know how many of you have ever attended proletarian rallies and assemblies. How have such assemblies always concluded? Invariably they conclude by imitating, albeit in proletarian consequence, what so many bourgeois assemblies trumpet, based on their bourgeois interests. In Central Europe, for instance, governing assemblies always used to begin or end with 'Three Cheers for the Kaiser!' And in turn every proletarian assembly concludes with something like 'Long Live International Revolutionary Social Democracy!' Just consider how hugely suggestive such a phrase must become when heard week in, week out, how it conjures a sense of unity amongst the masses, inevitably putting paid to all freedom in thinking. Such things embed themselves in the soul. Although this happens less and less now, in the past there were assemblies called by middle-class institutions to which social democrats were also invited. The chair of the assembly would say at the end of the gathering, 'I now request that the social democrats leave the room for a moment, since I am about to invite the members to stand and offer three cheers for the Kaiser.' And in turn there were proletarian assemblies, to which the gentry were sometimes admitted. And at the end the chair of the meeting would say, 'I now request the gentlemen of the bourgeois class to leave the room since we are going to offer three cheers for International Revolutionary Social Democracy.' Thus the unifying, uniform class consciousness that pervaded human souls was cast from one mould, as the very opposite of what sits deeper in human hearts—the opposite of the longing for individual freedom of thought, for individual configuring of the mind. That is the second thing.

The third thing that lives in the depths of the modern soul and urgently seeks to be realized is socialism: a socialism that we can simply characterize by saying that in the era of consciousness the modern soul seeks to feel itself as part of the social organism. There is a desire to found the social organism as such, as a human being to feel oneself an intrinsic part of this social organism, to stand within it in some way. In other words, a desire lives in people to be pervaded by the sense and feeling that as a human being whatever I do, I do in a way that tells me how much the social organism participates in me, and how much I participate in it. We live, after all, within the social organism. But, as I said, a sense for this social organism today is only present in subconscious regions of the soul.

When a painter paints a picture today, he will rightly say that he needs to be paid for it, since he has invested his art and craft in it. What is his art? Something that society, the social organism, first facilitated for him. Of course, it does depend on his karma, his former lives on earth. But people no longer believe in this, although they are naturally mistaken. But in so far as we do not credit the part played in our skills and ability by the individuality who descends at birth from higher regions, we are entirely dependent for our abilities on the social organism. But modern people take no account of this, remain unaware of it. And so, instead of a social sense, for the past four hundred years an increasingly egoistic, antisocial mode of thinking has arisen: the antisocial outlook which comes to expression especially in each person thinking first and foremost of himself, and trying to get as much as possible for himself from the social organism. Few people today have the sense that they must give back to the social organism everything they gained from it. Amongst the governing, gentrified classes, especially, the greatest conceivable egoism has gradually emerged in respect of culture and the life of the mind: an egoism that regards mere cultural delectation as something to which those who can procure it are particularly entitled. But we do not have any entitlement to cultural, spiritual delectation afforded us by the social organism unless we seek in turn, wherever we stand in the world, to give back to the social organism a corresponding equivalent. It is important to realize this.

Now the proletariat, which has been excluded from participation in the spiritual, cultural sphere of the social organism, and is harnessed to economic life and soulless capitalism, has simply drawn the ultimate consequence of this bourgeois egoism in the doctrine of 'added value'. The worker sees that it is *he* who in fact produces what is made in factories, in industry; and so he wishes to have the income obtained for it. He does not wish a part of this value to be deducted and accrue to others. And since he sees nothing more than the capitalist who puts him to work on the factory floor, naturally he believes that all added value benefits the capitalist. And therefore he rises up against the capitalist initially. But objectively speaking, of course, there is a quite different component also in what corresponds to this so-called added value. What is added value? It is everything produced through manual labour for which the labourer obtains no recompense. Imagine there were no added value: then everything would flow to the needs of the manual labourer. And then what would be lacking? Self-evidently, there would be no spiritual culture, no culture whatsoever. There would only be economic life, only what can arise and emerge through manual labour. Added value cannot accrue to manual labour itself, but can only be used in a way to which the manual labourer can agree. But this will only come about if the manual labourer is educated to understand the ways in which added value is used, the course it takes in society.

Here we touch on the worst violation of modern civil society. Factories and industry were established, trade was established, capital was circulated, labourers were set to work at machines and harnessed to the capitalist economy. They had to work. But no account was taken of wanting anything from the worker other than his labour. In a healthy social organism, besides the worker's labour, his rest must also be wanted and needed, the strength or energy that remains after he has done his work. The only justified capitalism is one that also has an interest in sparing the worker labour as much as in economic utilization of his work. The only justified capitalism is one that ensures that, after a certain number of working hours, the worker can in some way access culture and education of a universally human kind.

But to achieve this, culture and education must first be available. The middle-classes of society developed it and were therefore able to found all kinds of public education institutions. All kinds of cultural education programmes of this kind have been cooked up. But what did these cultural breweries teach the proletariat? Only that the gentry were dropping from their table crumbs of culture they had cooked up together. And naturally the workers were mistrustful of this. They thought, 'Ah, they want to gentrify me by feeding me the milk of their piety and manner of thinking in these places.' All these charitable movements and programmes were, by their very nature, often to blame for the upsurge of alarming realities in society. What is surfacing today rises from much graver depths than people usually realize. 'Give us the added value that belongs to us!' This is the egoistic principle now appearing as the ultimate consequence of gentrified egoism. The proletariat is drawing the ultimate consequences and, instead of the socialism dwelling in the underdepths of their souls, the intrinsically antisocial doctrine of added value has now appeared at the conscious forefront of their minds. You see, if each person pockets the 'added value' of goods, he is pocketing it for his own egoism.

And so today, my dear friends, we have a socialism that is not socialist, just as we have the quest for a content of consciousness that has no deeper reality but is just the result of the economic context of one class of people, coming to expression in the class consciousness of the proletariat. We have a quest for the spirit that denies the spirit, that has found its ultimate consequence in the materialistic view of history.

We must recognize these things; otherwise we will fail to understand what lives in the world today. The bourgeoisie has been very disinclined to gain understanding of these circumstances and, although the facts and realities speak forcefully and urgently to us today, they remain disinclined.

The only possible way to replace the antisocial strivings of the proletariat today with a truly social striving will be by trying to establish economic life upon its own healthy foundation as a sphere of the social organism with its own legislature and administration, unimpeded by state involvement. In other words, we must try to ensure that the state never engages in economic activity itself, in any field. And then the yearning deep in human souls for real socialism can develop in economic life. At the same time we must aspire to keep economic life separate and distinct from the life of the political state as such, which for its part makes no claim either on economic life nor on the life of culture, spiritual life *per se*: on cultural life, education and so forth. If this state refrains from interfering in either domain, if it embodies only the life of rights, then it expresses what underpins the relationship between one person and the other here in the physical world—the relationship in which all people are equal before the law. Only a state conducted in this way develops real freedom of thought. And as a third sphere of the healthy social organism, a self-founded life of spirit and culture must develop, one that can also draw sustenance from the reality of the spirit, and that must work its way through to a true science of the spirit. In the depths of human souls today, it is true to say, there lives already a questing for the healthy social organism, but this must in turn inevitably be threefold in nature.

Considering things as we have considered them today, we find that spiritual science should be taken very seriously, at a much deeper level than people are accustomed to when listening to a Sunday sermon—which is a comfortable, middle-class kind of attention. It is bourgeois when, alongside one's economic life which is largely concerned only with one's own little circle, or at least that's what people think, and alongside political life, the life of the state which one leaves to the state to take care of, people develop a little bit of cultural icing on the cake of existence. Depending on their degree of 'enlightenment' they attend church or devote themselves to theosophy or suchlike. In fact theosophy has assumed an eminently gentrified air in modern culture. It is hard to conceive of anything more middle-class than this modern theosophical movement, which grew very much out of bourgeois needs as a factional spiritual movement. We have been battling to elaborate something from this theosophical movement that could be informed by a modern consciousness befitting humanity, and place it into the world at large as an inclusive movement. But we have always met with resistance from the middle-class, factional element, which is deeply rooted in the superficial stratum of the human soul. And we have to get beyond this. Anthroposophic endeavour must be seen as something needed by the times we live in, something that should enlarge the scope of our interests not constrain them, that does not invite us just to gather in small circles and read lectures. Yes, it is good to read lecture cycles. I beg you not to conclude from what I say that you should stop doing so, but this alone is not enough. What you read in the cycles has to be led fully into human life, though not as many imagine, but by first seeking a connection, a relationship, with modern consciousness. I am *not* saying that we should stop reading lecture cycles, stop gathering in 'cliquish' groups and reading them. On the contrary, we should engage in this all the more, but then also take care that the content of these cycles is really integrated into our life forces. This will provide the best social sustenance for questing souls in the modern era. For that is the intention; that is also the intention of our building,[45] particularly in the artistic endeavour inherent in it. It is conceived very much as intrinsic to the modern era, and it is impossible to conceive of it in any other way. I wonder how much you have recognized that this building of ours, especially, is a product of the very greatest modernity in a social respect also, how the quest to engage with an up-to-the-minute modernity is integral to it. Recall this fact: we have here a building whose interior has no utilitarian purpose whatsoever, or at least a large part of its interior has none in terms of its own isolated structure. It has to stand in connection with the whole of the rest of the world order if it is to have any meaning at all. Even in the daytime it would be pitch-black up in the cupola, darkest night, if electric light did not fall upon it from without. The building is entirely dependent on what happens outside it as far as important matters are concerned such as whether we see anything inside it. It has been born from the very latest modernity, and therefore it has to be connected with what this modernity itself has to strive to attain, but now in a deeper, more inward way, not from a superficial level of the soul.

And so you might reflect upon a great many things that are connected with this building. It actually represents the most up-to-the-minute cultural life, and can only be properly understood by conceiving of it as a kind of comet that must drag its tail after it. The tail consists in this: that the felt content of anthroposophy, radiating from it, should live in human souls. And yet it could easily happen that people begin to relate to this building as a good many Catholics, leading Catholics in fact, related to modern astronomy when they ordained that comets were natural heavenly bodies as opposed to the 'rods' they had previously been thought to be, which some kind of spirit, conceived in sensory terms, had held out of the window of heaven.[46] A time arrived when Catholic leaders could no longer claim that comets were of an entirely different order from other heavenly bodies. But they thought of a way out of this problem. Very clever minds among them said, 'Yes, the comet consists of its nucleus and of its tail. We cannot deny that its nucleus is a heavenly body like any other, but the tail is not: the tail has the divine origin we previously ascribed to it.' Similarly one can imagine that people start to think that the building itself is solid and real enough but that they don't wish to entertain all the suspect and complex feelings that are meant to be connected with it as its tail. And yet this building and its tail belong together, and what is connected with it will have to be felt to be so.

Lecture 5

DORNACH, 2 MARCH 1919

YESTERDAY we tried to examine the modern social movement from a particular angle. We found it necessary, when seeking understanding of any movement, to give close study to what lives in the forefront of its adherents' minds and in the minds of the rest of their contemporaries, what lives in their ordinary consciousness, and what on the other hand is occurring in the depths of the soul, in subconscious regions. Here we considered three impulses at work in the modern proletarian movement: first its materialistic view of history; then what workers have learned from their leaders about the class warfare that supposedly underlies all historical events; and then we also focused on something that has had such a decisive impact on proletarian souls: the 'added value' theory, as it is known. We saw how these things lie uppermost in the consciousness of the modern proletarian. But in the depths below, something quite different is stirring. As opposed to the illusion that the proletarian harbours today, that all history simply reflects economic processes and that culture is merely a kind of vapour rising from this reality, the worker, along with all of modern humanity, thirsts for a certain spiritual insight into the world. But he does not know this; he is unaware that in the subconscious depths of his soul he thirsts for spiritual knowledge. And what stirs in these subconscious regions, and is masked by something quite different at the surface, often rumbles and erupts in the wildest instincts.

Similarly, when the modern proletarian invokes the phrase 'class conflict', he does not realize that he is only trying to conceal with it another deep longing in the underdepths of modern soul life, the impulse for freedom of thought. On the journey from the subconscious to the conscious mind, the quest for freedom of thinking is transformed into its opposite. The search for freedom in thinking underlies the most extreme adherence to authority to which mere 'class consciousness' testifies. And true socialism, for which our era yearns in the depths, comes to expression really in a kind of opposite of socialism, in the endeavour to egoistically pocket all 'added value'.

If we don't understand this secret of the modern proletarian movement, the social impulses at work today will be hidden from us. Yesterday we looked at these things, and now I'd like to lead on to a consideration of a few truths relating to them.

By seeking to look more deeply into what is actually happening, we can gain a very particular relationship to global movements, including those of today. As you know, Bolshevism is a modern social movement in its most radical and extreme form. It is a social methodology little different in content to what other forms of radical socialism intend. If you study the reality and not just the theory of history, it is helpful to examine how certain currents in humanity's evolution come to their most radical expression, for it is here that we can best understand what is otherwise also present, more concealed but no less influential, where radicalism is less dominant. If we want to grasp the historical conclusions that history itself has drawn in the terrible events of today, this historical outcome in Bolshevism, we will need to survey modern culture a little.

If you ask who these Bolsheviks are really, various names will be cited, predominant among whom are of course Lenin and Trotsky.[47] But I'd like to tell you about a third Bolshevik whose name might somewhat surprise you, but from one point of view he has to be called a genuine Bolshevik. This is Johann Gottlieb Fichte.[48] I have often spoken about him to you, and have even tried to illumine his biography from a somewhat deeper perspective.[49] We have reflected here too on some of Fichte's chief ideas. It cannot be denied that he was one of the most energetic thinkers of modern times. But he also expressed his socialist leanings in summarized form, in *The Closed Commercial State*. If we study what reality would arise from Fichte's view of ideal social conditions, we would have to say that it would manifest as Bolshevism. Actually, what Trotsky writes is sometimes very reminiscent, almost identical word for word in so far as such divergent things can be so, of what Fichte writes in *The Closed Commercial State*.

Fichte of course is a long-dead Bolshevik; but this is precisely what can invite us to examine this fact a little more closely. We must regard Fichte as a very lonely thinker who arrived at lofty philosophical ideas and who turned his thoughts also to various social injustices, as he saw them, and to how a just society might eventually emerge. Out of his inner soul he weaves a picture of the social order, conjuring a structuring of society roughly in the same way as modern Russian Bolshevism does, and as its successors will, in its own violent manner. I can understand that many, moved by various injustices still of course existing in society today, will feel fascinated by the very simple outlooks expressed in Fichte's *The Closed Commercial State*. I don't need to go into any more detail about this text here since it is enough to recall what Bolshevism is doing, and frame it in the cultured words of a philosopher, and then you have *The Closed Commercial State* by Fichte. And this very fact can illustrate why it is right and proper to establish the threefold nature of the healthy social organism, of which I have often spoken.

What is the real meaning and purpose of this threefold structure? In public lectures I have suggested how this mode of social thinking differs from others. I have said that if we examine the reality that has been created here and there in particular state structures, if we study the ideas that socialist thinkers are seeking to realize in practice, we can easily have a sense that a kind of medieval superstition has taken hold deep in their souls. It is as if human souls had a certain craving for superstition, and when this is driven out of them in one form, it seeks to take root again in another. And this is why I am reminded of Part II of Goethe's *Faust* both in relation to various aspects already existing in society, and also to what socialist thinkers intend. I am thinking of the scene where Wagner creates the homunculus. The homunculus is to be made from mechanical components arranged according to prosaic, rational principles. The alchemists, who are regarded today as superstitious people, thought such a thing was perfectly possible, and contrasted the artificial creation of a little human, the homunculus, with the origin of a real human organism. One cannot compose an actual human organism from its constituents but must create the conditions that, in a sense, allow it to arise by itself. In science, people believe that they have overcome this alchemical superstition, yet it still flourishes in views of society. There people try to create an artificial social order from all kinds of constituents of human will.

This mode of thinking is diametrically opposed to the one we propose here, drawing on spiritual-scientific foundations. The outlook we propose seeks to shed all social superstition and, in practical terms, to answer the question as to what conditions must be created so that—instead of some person or other being able to realize a socialist ideal through his particular ingenuity—people can create the necessary social forms in reciprocal activity together in society.

But here we find that this social organism, just like the natural organism, must actually consist of three relatively independent spheres. Just as the human head, which chiefly bears the sense organs, has a particular relationship with the external world through these sense organs and is centralized in, or founded on, itself; and just as, in turn, the rhythmic system of lungs and breathing is centralized in itself, as is likewise the metabolic system, these three spheres or systems interacting in their relative autonomy: so it is fundamentally necessary for the social order to be tripartite, and for each of its three domains to have relative autonomy. The autonomous, self-founded spiritual and cultural organism, the autonomous organism of the political state in its narrower sense, and the autonomous economic organism, must all work alongside each other, each of these entities having their own legislature and forms of administration arising from their own contexts, and the circumstances and forces at work in them. This may sound abstract, but it is precisely what can structure the whole of society to produce the health of the social organism from the interaction and collaboration of these different spheres. It is therefore not a question of contriving a fixed model of how the social organism should be shaped. In the social domain our thinking, you see, does not extend far enough to be able to propose the social organism's structure. An individual can as little realize the structure of the social organism as a person could ever learn to speak if he were first to awaken on a lonely island without any social context. The single human being cannot weave a social context by himself. All social co-existence arises reciprocally, and will only be truly harmonious as human mutuality regulated by these threefold principles. It is only by recognizing this truly practical way of shaping actual life that we can come to understand how someone like Johann Gottlieb Fichte came to contrive a social system whose realization would in fact lead to Bolshevism.

What kind of a figure is Johann Gottlieb Fichte? He was one of the characteristic thinkers of modern times, in a sense the man who also developed and honed thinking—which has evolved in the course of time, has changed in character as you can see from my *Riddles of Philosophy*—in the most energetic way and gave it its purest form. A figure such as Fichte can show us what thinking becomes if we seek to draw it entirely from itself alone, from the I. And if we apply this pure thinking, in its intrinsic nature, to the structure of society too, we obtain the picture that Fichte gave us in *The Closed Commercial State*. But we have to recognize that thinking such as this, Fichtean thinking, is completely unsuited to finding social structure. Thinking drawing upon the impulse of the I is not able to discern social structure, just as a single person alone could not invent speech. Social structure can only be found by first bringing human beings into mutual relationship and interaction, so that they find social structure in their interconnection. To some degree we have to stop short before certain things relating to social structure, only pursuing the path to the point where you show how people must relate to one another if the social organism is to be realized in their collaboration. This is thinking that corresponds to reality, to actual experience. Fichte's thinking is born from the pure I, as is Bolshevik thinking, albeit in somewhat different form. It is basically antisocial because it is born only from the manifestations of the I, and specifically does not arise in the life of human community. The community life of the proletariat adopted this form of thought on authority, but it is dictated by the leaders of their movement, and it is important to recognize this.

This begs the question as to what is added to the individual's inner life by this life of the community, in the social domain. Here we have to recognize very clearly where this purest form of thinking in Fichte leads us. If you try to read Fichte's books without preparation or previous study of philosophy, just picking them up as you might read the newspaper or books that are easier to digest, or even perhaps current academic works as they are today, you will find them very difficult to follow: you will get the sense that you are being skewered on these thoughts. They are so energetic but developed in such an abstract way. What Fichte elaborates strikes most people as a cat's cradle of abstract thoughts.

Why is this? It is because this thinking is pure thinking, of a kind that the soul weaves above and beyond any experience of the world, that is woven out of itself. If you study Fichte's *Theory of Knowledge* you pass from one clause to the next in lofty abstract heights so that you often cannot tell why you should be concerning yourself with them at all since they say absolutely nothing to you. You can leaf a long way through Fichte's *Theory of Knowledge* and you will learn that 'the I posits itself'. This thought is elaborated over many pages to start with, followed by 'the I posits the not-I'—again elaborated over many pages. Then comes the third thing, 'The I posits itself as defined by the not-I and the not-I as defined by the I.' And by this time you have almost reached the end of his *Theory of Knowledge,* which takes these thoughts and elaborates them in a very broad and wide-ranging way. You will say, 'Well, that is of no interest to me whatsoever, for really it is all hollow and abstract.' And yet if you trace Fichte's biography, his life and endeavours, as I presented them to you some time ago, you gain real respect for Fichte, for his quest for pure thinking.

To what is this remarkable contradiction due? It comes from the fact that in the course of human evolution it became necessary at a particular point to reach this pure thinking filled only by thoughts. Human thinking has otherwise only been filled with images, especially always in ancient times as I explained again yesterday. Figures such as Fichte, Schelling and Hegel, by contrast, have thought in pure thoughts, thoughts without pictures. The ancient Greeks could never have thought like this, nor the Romans, nor was it possible in medieval times since the Scholastics, despite all their abstraction, had a quite different quality of thinking.

What then was the purpose of developing this abstract thinking in the course of modern times? It arose because people needed to exert themselves. Great inner exertion is required to raise oneself in the Fichtean sense to such levels of abstraction, to elaborate abstractions which strike the man or woman in the street as useless, devoid of all real experience. It is true that it is. And yet it is important to reach this abstract level, to pass through this stage. After taking this first step into such abstractions, one soon develops the inner impulsivity of soul life a little further to get beyond them and enter spiritual life. There is no healthier path in modern mysticism than to pass through this energetic thinking, and this is why the capacity for it first had to be achieved. The next step on from, and through, this energetic thinking is to come to a real experience of the spiritual. In the passage of history this naturally all happens very slowly, but that is the path humanity is treading. And this longing, which in fact holds sway in all people today, to pass on from abstraction to the life of spirit, lies secretly also as a force rooted in the underdepths of the proletarian movement.

The proletarian does not believe that there are spiritual forces at work in history but only economic ones. Using the dullest perception, he observes these, and regards them as the only factor in history. He thinks that the life of spirit, culture, is just a superstructure, an ideology, a reflection of external economic factors. He thinks like this because when a person looks inward in modern times he sees only abstractions, having lost the old, atavistic visions. He finds only abstract thoughts within him, and they contain no reality for him—which could only be found by taking the further step I just described. For this reason people seek the reality they inwardly long for only in the external world. And because the worker has been harnessed to merely economic life since the advent of capitalism, he seeks this reality there.

What will the next, natural, inevitable step be? People will learn to see that the economic order as such does not ultimately offer any real driving force. As history continues, by contrast to this historical materialism, a force will develop within people to penetrate to the spirit. What comes to expression in historical materialism is only a caricature of the longing deep in human souls.

And similarly, below class consciousness lies the strength of the single human individual who seeks within him for inner content, and this comes to expression—because of a sense of inner emptiness, a lack at present of discernible content—in his adhering to his whole class, feeling strengthened by this whole human context.

Thus all the impulses that today prevail at the surface of the social movement arise from a hidden source, as I have described. And at the time when Fichte was writing, which was not yet ripe for the endeavours of spiritual science, the only thinking that could appear was one that still awaits the approach of the world of spirit and is also of no use for external reality. The thinking that should really be applied to the spiritual world leads—when radically, consistently, violently applied to the external sense world—not to the support and cultivation of sense reality but to its destruction. I have often spoken to you about the functions of evil,[50] describing the forces that are really at work in what we call human evil. I said that if we go one level higher, from our sensory plane to the next adjoining spiritual plane, our spiritual vision can teach us what is actually at work in evil. You see, if the powers active in thieves, robbers and murderers were not wrongly expressed here in the sense world but were metamorphosed, transformed to a higher plane, they would be fully justified. They belong there. Evil is good in the wrong place. It is only because the ahrimanic powers press down into our world what really belongs in a quite different world, that evil takes its particular form. And thus a destructive thinking arises—not one that can await fulfilment from the world of spirit—when a social ideal is spun from human inwardness.

This can give us insight into the difference between all the numerous abstractions that prevail today and what we seek here as a really practical grasp of the social organism. What this stimulates in human community, what people then develop together if proper community is established, does not manifest abstract thought. Abstract thoughts come to expression when the human being is really genuinely lonely, not when people are together. In the latter case hidden, mysterious imaginations come to expression instead. And only these mysterious imaginations, when realized, give the social organism a fitting form and structure. This is why the advances made in modern spiritual science are connected with the only wholesome, healing impulses for a socialist world order. The deficiencies and harm, the unhealthy nature of the modern social order, arises from the Fichtean way in which it seeks to forge from merely inner demands something that can only be grasped experientially.

If we study the efforts of modern times to make the state increasingly centralized, it becomes clear that this has inevitably led to convulsions and disruptions in the social organism. The reasons for these convulsions and disturbances lie deeper than is recognized by those who see the modern proletarian movement only as a movement for fair wages or bread. For even if a movement for fair wages and bread is needed, it is not a matter just of rearranging salaries or bread distribution but of *how* people seek to do so. And the reflections we have been engaging in today can show how we should approach such questions.

Let us consider the question of added value that we came to at the end of yesterday's lecture. Anyone who has witnessed the proletarian revolution knows how incisive this question has been after its leaders implanted it as an idea in workers' souls. What is this 'added value theory' based on? Really on what I described the day before yesterday at the public lecture in Basel:[51] that an untruth does indeed hold sway nowadays in the relationship between employer and employee, though neither the employer nor the employee are aware of this untruth in their conscious mind. The fact is masked and hidden. But even though people are unaware of it, it still acts in the soul as a feeling, it rises up from subconscious depths.

Let's recall the most important thing here. The employee today has a very specific relationship to his employer, which he feels to be unworthy of him even if his conscious mind may sometimes see it very differently. Inwardly he feels this relationship to be degrading to him because it means he has to sell his labour to the employer or entrepreneur as any other commodity. In the secret depths of his soul he feels that nothing that is part of the human being should be sold. When a person sells his labour, his whole being in reality accompanies it.[52] We have already discussed this in the past.

The question could be put as follows, and this is usually how it is put in socialist thinking: What is the right way of recompensing someone for their labour? Social ideals are usually concerned with paying full remuneration for manual labour, for a person's work. But in fact the reality has to be seen quite differently. Anyone who understands economics will recognize that human labour cannot be exchanged for anything else at all. It cannot be paid for with any commodity or any commodity token such as money. It is not a reality but only an imaginary one, albeit realized in actuality, that a worker works and then is paid money for his labour. The truth is masked here, creates a kind of lie. What actually happens is quite different. In the social organism it seems that the worker brings his labour to market and the employer purchases this labour with the salary he pays. But this is not true at all. In the economic realm one cannot do anything other than exchange one commodity for another—commodity of course seen here in the very broadest terms. All economic activity consists in reality only in the exchange of goods. But what is a commodity in actual fact? A piece of land is, in itself, not yet a commodity. The coal in the ground is not yet a commodity. A commodity can only be something connected with human activity, either inwardly altered in nature by this activity or transported by it from one place to another. If you consider these two possible attributes, you cover everything that can in any way be called a commodity. The nature of commodities has been much disputed, but if you understand economics, you realize that this is the only definition of any worth.

Now, in the modern social organism, the circulation of goods has been fused or combined with other things, and this has driven this modern social organism to its revolutionary convulsions. Today it is thought—and this too is realized fantasy—not only that goods are exchanged for other goods, but also that goods are exchanged for human labour, as in the wage relationship; and furthermore, it is thought that goods, or their token, money, are exchanged for something that cannot be a commodity unless it has been changed or worked upon by human beings—land for instance. Land in itself is not subject to the economic process. Objects figuring in the economic process are obtained *upon* the land through human activity, but the land itself cannot be traded in the economic process. As far as the land and soil are concerned in the economy, in the social organism altogether, all we can say is that one person or another has a *right* to exclusive use of this land. This right to the land is what has real meaning for the social organism. The land and soil itself are not a commodity, but commodities are raised upon it. And this is governed by the right that the owner has to the land. So if you purchase a piece of land, that is, trade it for a commodity, you are exchanging a commodity for a right. And this is the case too when people buy patents.

Here we meet the conflation that has caused such havoc, between the purely political state and economic life, for which no other remedy exists but to separate the two. We must let economic life hold sway on its own terms purely in the production of goods, circulation of goods, consumption of goods, in associative life in which production, consumption, the various professional interests that unite people, enter into the right relationship. But within these associations and associative groups economic activity only operates as the digestion does in our organism; and then, on the other hand, this digestion is engaged by the independent lung and heart system which has its own relationship with the outer world. What lives in the digestive system is further received and encompassed by the independent heart and respiratory process. Thus what is rightly rooted in economic life must, from a particular source, be discerned and established as independent. That means that political matters, and all that comes to expression in the life of rights and other such things, must have a relative independence and autonomy alongside economic life.

If one comprehends this, one also sees the untruth existing in the relationship between employer and employee, apparent in the illusion that the employer is remunerating the employee for his labour. This labour is not directly paid for at all, but only indirectly. What we have here is a certain apparent law, but one that has become violation, economic violation, by means of which the employer compels the worker to station himself at the machine or in a factory—compels him not entirely openly but in another guise. What is actually exchanged here is not labour against commodity or commodity token, i.e. money, but output: the goods that the worker produces. And so what is really exchanged is a small portion of these goods, that the employer gives the worker, for the goods produced, thus commodity for commodity. And the untruth lies in the illusion that goods are being exchanged for labour. The modern proletarian senses this as a secret wrong, and feels his human dignity is violated, expressing this in terms of the fact that he produces a certain amount of goods but the employer allows him only a percentage of their value.

The proper relationship between the employee and the employer cannot belong in the sphere of the economic process at all but only in the sphere of the political state as a rights relationship. That is the important thing. On the foundation of economic life, on the one hand, and on that of the independent life of rights on the other, this economic life is determined from two directions. From one perspective economic life is dependent on natural factors independent of human activity. For instance, as I explained in the public lectures in Basel, the natural yield of, say, a wheat crop possible due to the soil in one region will differ from that of another, and accordingly different corresponding amounts of human labour will be required in each. These are the natural bases that affect economic activity on the one hand, and on the other have implications for labour governed by the life of rights, which must establish a fitting relationship here between employer and employee.

Now people with a merely superficial view of things will say that this is already the case, for such things are governed by the employment contract. Yet what use is this contract, my dear friends, if it governs what is in fact a concealed lie? The employment contract governs the relationship between employer and employee in regard to labour and remuneration. But the contract would only rightly apply if it made quite plain that it relates not to wages but to the manner in which employer and employee are to share the output that is produced. And then the worker—and this is the important thing—would recognize that it is not possible to do without the creation of added value. But he must consider how this added value arises. It must not be built into a relationship founded on a lie. Then he will come to see that without added-value creation one cannot have any culture or spiritual life, nor any rights state, for all this flows from added value. And if the social organism is healthy, all this will follow from the threefold social organism.

This outlook is of course one we could speak about for days on end, as we almost have done now; yet in the process we keep uncovering new details and aspects which should make it more comprehensible, since we can gain inklings of every specific question that might arise, and the practical task of threefolding in attempting to answer it.

The following, for instance, is one of the things that must be considered above all: in economic life goods are exchanged; and the life of the political state, in the narrower sense, adjoins this economic life. In the sphere of human community, in the life of rights, the political state limits or defines working hours. And so while economic life is on the one hand dependent on natural foundations as we saw, on the other it is also dependent on decisions made in the rights sphere—thus about working hours, for instance, and the relationship between labour and the individual in matters such as his strength, his frailty, his age. There cannot be such a thing as a fixed length of the working day but in reality only an upper and lower limit. All such things are conditions that affect economic life from one direction, just as natural foundations affect it from the other.

If the social organism thus becomes healthier, then it will put an end to the really dreadful way in which remuneration is determined by economic factors themselves, so that wages rise when business is booming and can be reduced when it is not. This will be turned on its head: business will boom as an effect of the worker's salary and vice versa.

Ground rent, today largely dependent on the price of goods, the market price of goods produced on the land, can also illustrate these changes very clearly. The right and healthy relationship would be the opposite: when the right of use, expressed in ground rent, in turn affects market price. Often threefolding will lead to the very reverse of current conditions, which have caused our revolutionary convulsions. The whole of life will run differently.

What must we consider above all in the relationship between economic life and the political state in its narrower sense? One of these things you will easily ascertain yourselves: it is something often regarded as unpleasant—taxation. All that matters as regards taxation is that we can really clearly discern how taxes must flow from added value, and that, in democratic political co-existence, we remain aware of the life of the political organism just as we remain aware of economic life as we buy and sell, thus clearly perceiving the reality of this economic relationship arising from human needs. And this in turn will lead to something indicative of the healthy social organism, and the opposite of what exists today. I'm not saying that we should change the taxation laws. Under present circumstances, there is much that cannot be altered, or can only be so by shifting what is wrong elsewhere. But a vital effect of the healthy threefold social organism will be that people develop a quite different view of particular aspects of society. They will come to see that the income a person procures is of no significance for the life of society as such, for human life in the social organism. As we procure our income, we detach ourselves from the social organism, and this can be a matter of great indifference to the social organism. The income someone earns has no importance whatsoever for its functions. Instead, a person becomes a social being by spending. Only as he spends, does someone start to act with social relevance. And taxation must start precisely when we spend—I am not referring here to indirect taxation but expenditure tax, which is something quite different. It is beyond the scope of this lecture to give you all the details here, although the details can of course be worked out: it requires a deeper study of economics than we can engage in here. But I can point to some of the aspects involved.

In healthy economic life, with its separation from the other spheres of the social organism, it becomes apparent that it costs more to grow wheat, say, in one region than another due to soil conditions. And it may be that associative life alone cannot compensate for this difference. But it can be corrected entirely through the life of rights, and in such a case it could come about entirely by itself that those who purchase wheat at a cheaper price, and thus spend less, must pay a higher tax than those who have to pay more for the wheat, and must thus spend more.

If the rights state properly regulates laws in economic life, and if these laws are therefore not just an embodiment of vested economic interests—for instance because the Farmers' Federation wields power in parliament and the legislature—but are determined by those whose particular task it is to create laws and rights affecting human interrelationships, then it will be possible to fully and properly regulate economic life. I am speaking generally and in the abstract. These things would have to be worked out in detail. But that broadly is the nature of the tax relationship between economic life and political life.

The relationship between economic life and the life of rights on the one hand, and the life of culture on the other, is however one that can only be founded on trust and understanding. While taxation must be compulsory, even in the healthy social organism, the funding of spiritual life and culture can on the other hand only be voluntary, since the latter must be founded entirely on the human spirit, and accord with the spirit of our humanity. It must be completely emancipated from everything else. And then it will, in turn, work back upon everything else in the strongest and profoundest way.

I have only given you outlines of how the social organism should function if it is to be healthy. This threefolding is not an arbitrary invention but simply what we can observe when we study the deeper forces at work in human evolution, which have become active today and will, whether or not we prefer otherwise, be realized in the next ten, twenty or thirty years. It can only be a matter of how they are realized. I have observed these forces and formulated them as an outlook, a way of seeing things. And it is generally true that historical insights can help us to perceive what is seeking realization. This is not an infringement of our freedom, for freedom relates to something quite different. It is as little a violation of our freedom as it is to say we can't grasp hold of the moon although we might like to. Our freedom is realized in correspondence with necessities that lie equally in the natural and in the historical process of evolution.

LECTURE 6

DORNACH, 7 MARCH 1919

There is a curious paragraph in the lecture which Kurt Eisner[53] gave recently to the Basel students' association. He starts with the odd question as to whether the current state of humanity as we experience it is a reality or whether it might not be merely a dream; whether our human experience nowadays might be a kind of dreamed reality. The paragraph in question runs as follows:

> Am I mistaken—or is my vision clear and true—that there is, deep in our existence a longing, seeking to come to light, that the life we are compelled to live today might be only the invention of some evil spirit? Imagine if you will a great thinker who knew nothing of our era, and who lived around 2000 years ago. Imagine he had dreamed how the world might appear in two millennia. With the liveliest possible imagination he could not have conceived of a world such as the one we are now condemned to live in. What exists is in reality, after all, the only utopia and what we desire, what lives in our minds as longing, is the deepest, ultimate reality. Everything else is a ghastly spectre. We confuse dream with waking. Our task is to shake off this old dream of our modern social existence. Just look at the war: can we conceive of a human mind that could have dreamed up such a thing? If this war has not been what we call 'real', perhaps we have been dreaming and are now waking up.

> We are a society in which human beings, despite their railways, steam engines and electric lights, still only perceive a small part of this planet upon which we have been born.

That was the feeling to which Kurt Eisner gave expression in Basel shortly before he died. Thus today the nature of reality forces us to ask whether we are awake or only dreaming. Is this reality of ours real at all? And actually it would be very good if people today could ask this or similar questions more often, more extensively. You see it is vital that people should be able to perceive reality in everything that they encounter in the world around them. We have emphasized in various ways how important it is no longer to view what the world needs, what society in particular needs, only in terms of the old habits of thought acquired over the past few centuries through to our own time. A clear view of things will show us that these very habits of thought have led us into catastrophe. In cultivating them, people often consider themselves to be pragmatists. And yet they take their point of departure from the grimmest abstraction, then seek to make such abstractions reality. But precisely because these habits of thought have flowed into and given rise to the reality that has been created, it has gradually become an unreal configuration, incapable of sustaining life. We live within this social context, true enough, and regard it as our reality, but it has no real life-giving powers.

These are things that cannot be strongly enough accentuated today, and which must be clearly stated by all who look realities squarely in the face. Such facts and realities, albeit initially unfolding only in the daily outer world, speak to us in a way that clearly demonstrates how healing of modern conditions can only come through impulses from the world of spirit. What has grown alien from the spiritual world in recent centuries, running its affairs, if you like, without any account of the world of spirit, now finds itself in a cul-de-sac from which it cannot get out again. And to keep thinking that one can pursue business as usual with the same methods that drove us into this catastrophe is a kind of mindlessness. What have we witnessed after all? We have seen a humanity that believed it had created the highest material civilization. Think back to how comfortable things appeared before August 1914. Recall how easily we could travel back and forth from one country to another as long as we were members of the class and culture that could afford such things. Recall how easy it had become to communicate, across national boundaries, by telegraph and telephone, with the furthest-flung places in the world. If we think of everything that humanity called 'civilization' and then of what has become of it in Europe since August 1914, and the conditions we are now living in today, it will be fairly apparent, won't it my dear friends, that the one and the other are connected: that our present conditions were already implicit in the 'comfortable', 'civilized' way we lived until August 1914. As I put it in the Vienna lecture that I gave before the war, this sickness was already present then as a social cancer, a carcinoma in human society.[54] It ought really to be acknowledged that, at a time when things were still so 'civilized' and 'comfortable', when everything seemed to flatter human desires—as long as people's social class and status gave them the means to pursue them—spiritual science was already elaborating a clear view of reality that had to be expressed as a sickness in society. We were living already in a sick, not a healthy society. We had long been offering a cure for this sickness in the form of an anthroposophic way of thinking. And indeed, the only cure will be to recognize that anything that does not seek this mode of thinking, with its receptivity to real spirit, will be more or less just charlatanism. We have to pour reality again into what humanity is at present only dreaming. Where shall we find it? It is not found in what the 'pragmatists' draw their ideas from. It is present only where spirit is perceived. And it is this that must be the source of principles and impulses that can flow into society. And so we must always point to this context, this interconnection of things.

In the context of these lectures I have often mentioned the name of Fritz Mauthner to you.[55] He published two volumes which he entitled *Dictionary of Philosophy* and there classified modern thinking under a series of headings, listed in alphabetical order, along with his own distinctive brand of sometimes vitriolic critique. He writes there among other things of the state, the *res publica*. Fritz Mauthner arrived by his own process of thinking at a kind of answer about what the state actually is. He formulates this definition, and nothing more: 'The state is a necessary evil.' People can't deny its necessity, you see, but it has become apparent to some that the social structure we nowadays call the state ultimately has led to the conditions in which we now live. And so they call it a necessary evil, since its dire character, in its modern form, is apparent to them. But we must now ask how we might arrive at a positive idea of the state as opposed to this merely negative one.

If someone highlights the negative, we should try to point to the positive, to something affirmative, shouldn't we? So if someone says the state is a necessary evil, he is offering us the negative opposite of something, and we can try to discover what this positive something might be. And here spiritual science shows us a very remarkable fact. We only understand the state, don't we, when we gain insight into the legal structure that holds sway in it, and the way conditions of ownership, labour and so on are regulated; and when we then compare and contrast this legal edifice with something else.

My dear friends, in my various books and lectures you have become acquainted with the world of spirit, with relationships that unfold in the spiritual world in the periods we pass through between death and a new birth. And the question is this: in what way do these soul relationships between death and a new birth relate to the legal conditions that are established on the physical plane within the social state? To this question comes the reply that the structure of the state is the precise opposite of human relationships in the world of spirit. And this can give a true picture of the state. People who are quite unaware of a world of spirit cannot gain any picture of the state either, since they have nothing but negative definitions and regulations about interpersonal relations. Positive definitions are the ones that arise when one soul relates to another in the spiritual world. If, with this in view, you read the chapter in my book *Theosophy*[56] about the soul realm, you will discover that a certain kind of regulation of soul-to-soul relationships occurs there, and continues also into what we can call spirit land; and you will see that these relationships are governed by forces that pass between souls and which can be termed the interaction of sympathy and antipathy. In this chapter in *Theosophy* you will see how sympathy and antipathy bring about a certain relationship between one soul and the other in the world of spirit; you will see that in the spiritual world all depends on inwardness, that is, on what works between souls through the forces of sympathy and antipathy. On the physical plane the workings between souls of the forces of antipathy are concealed by human corporeality; and because of this, because the true, essential relationship between one soul and the other is hidden here on the physical plane, in the sphere of the state on the physical plane the most outward conceivable thing must happen: legal regulation. Whereas our account of the world of the spirit must speak of an unfolding of the most inward powers of the soul, what can live in the state on earth can only be the most externalized aspect of interpersonal relationships. This state is not healthy if it tries to establish anything other than the most externalized legal relationship. For this reason anything that does not involve the most externalized legal relationship between one person and another must be excluded from state jurisdiction. And the sphere of spirit, administration of cultural affairs, must stand in opposition and contrast to the true sphere of the state, thus defined; and in turn also to purely economic activity, the third member of the social organism. Whereas the state *per se* represents the complete opposite of the world of spirit, our life of spirit and culture, as I explained before from a different perspective, is a kind of perpetuation of what we experienced in the real spiritual world before we descended into earthly life at birth. What we experience here in religion, education, art, science and so forth, as well as the connections we develop in this sphere with other people, is the earthly perpetuation—though only a reflection, a mere mirroring—of our actual spiritual life prior to birth.

Our economic activity, by contrast, that involves us in what is usually called our 'material' life, is in fact the cause and origin of much that we will experience after we cross the threshold of death, thus in life after death. But the state has no relationship with the life of spirit, being the precise opposite of it. And so, if we wish to understand the present age with its dire realities, we must learn to see how necessary it is to take account of spiritual realities in order to gain insight into external reality. Antipathy and sympathy work together in the world of spirit. The antipathies we still retain in the world of spirit when we descend again to earthly existence at birth, and what we must still work through because of these antipathies we retained in the spiritual world, come to expression here as spiritual culture. As human beings we learn to understand each other through speech, and by this means in a sense to forge a spiritual bond between ourselves and others because, by understanding speech, we must overcome certain antipathies that we brought with us from the spiritual world. We learn to speak to one another in certain ideas, to have thoughts in common in a shared art, a shared religious confession. In doing so we overcome certain antipathies that we had for one another in the world of spirit. And in economic life here, too, we learn to be dependent on one another, to work for one another, to exchange benefits for benefits with each other in economic activity; and by this means we lay the foundations for certain sympathies which should unfold in the life after death between souls whose ordinary karma has not already created a bond of attraction here.

But it is so hard for us to accustom ourselves to this that, in respect of the life of culture, it becomes necessary for us gradually to come to understand a whole new language. Really people would like the old languages to go on being spoken. They think it will be alright if they continue to speak the old kind of language. There are unctuous prophets who propound their outlooks today—I have spoken before about such an outlook. A figure, for instance, who is highly regarded in our time,[57] tells us that this world war showed how people live in a kind of external organization, but without inwardly getting close to each other. And so this war has, he says, produced a throw-back to the old barbarism. And to save us from this barbarism, he offers us what you might call feeling phrases that tell us to return to a sort of inner life of spirit. But this is not what is needed today, dear friends;

it is no good urging people to become good Christians again, to learn to love their fellow men and forge an inner bond between each other. It is much more important to develop a power of spirit that enables us really to master outward conditions, to give external circumstances a real structure so that the social order comes to life, becomes life-sustaining. If we are really honest we cannot say that people today are ailing first and foremost because they do not believe in the spirit. There are enough people who do; and actually every village has its little church where, I imagine, there is much talk of the spirit. Even those who oppose the spirit have a certain respect for it. It is still second nature for people to speak of the spirit in some way or other. People like Anzengruber, who says 'I swear by God in heaven that I am an atheist',[58] are by no means so uncommon, whether or not they put it quite like that. But whether or not people speak of the spirit, or even believe in it, is not the thing that matters. What is important is that the spirit should *work* in and through all material life, so that people recognize that matter can never exist without spirit.

Now we could cite a great many more variations on this theme of the relationship as perceived today between material life and spiritual life. Basically, people have the feeling that to embrace the spirit one must turn one's back on outward material existence. Ultimately this is connected with the fact that in modern times we have so many ruptured lives, so many people who are dissatisfied with daily life. My dear friends, I am not speaking of you particularly. But nevertheless I'll say this: there is nothing uninteresting in life as long as a healthy social organism exists into which a person can integrate himself in accordance with his karma. Really no one in the world has any reason to regard a particular current in life as being less valuable than any other. But we must heal the social organism so that the lowliest labourer is as connected with a life of culture and spirit as someone who by chance is able to employ himself in spiritual concerns. It does the greatest injury to modern society to have closed circles within which special interests develop, which are more or less unavailable to others. Try to gain a sense of how, in our era, closed groups have formed in religion, art and everything else in middle-class life, and how proletarian circles are excluded from all this. Yes, the ruling classes arrange 'public events' for them, found 'workers' cultural institutes' and so on. But what is dispensed in this way has arisen from the sensibilities of the middle classes. If the proletarian is to embrace them he embraces a lie, since only what issues from shared experience can create a shared life of culture. There is no common, shared experience if one person has to stand for eight hours a day at his machine or conveyor belt—as you see, I'm already assuming an eight-hour day—while someone else can construct himself a social and cultural life within his privileged class, and then let crumbs fall from his table for the worker when the latter finishes his eight-hour stint: little remnants of things whose inmost structure and configuration can really only be understood by someone who belongs to the ruling classes.

Within these ruling classes, it is possible to speak—to take a concrete example—of the Sistine Madonna, because these people have a certain basic education. I have led groups of workers around in galleries and was able to see for myself what a lie it is to present to the modern labourer something resembling the feelings which the modern middle classes can have in response to such a painting. This just can't be done. But if you try to anyway, all that you're doing is creating a lie, since there is no common, shared life between the classes. And where there is none, you can't speak in a language that both will really understand. The ruling classes have until now been destined to gain something, say in art, which can take root in their whole feeling about life. Through the whole way in which humanity has lived and evolved hitherto, something like the Sistine Madonna has become a gift to and for the ruling classes, remaining initially incomprehensible to the others. So here we first have to look for a language that both can share; that is, we must first make efforts to find a really universally human life of education and culture. And our schools and universities are of course far removed from such universality.

It will not be enough to realize something that is so often sought: a comprehensive education. It will be necessary to teach in a quite different way from how children are taught today, that is, in a way that can only come about within a free life of spirit and culture as a sphere of the healthy social organism. You see, in his deepest core the proletarian does not understand what is taught nowadays in general education.

You will find a contradiction here, and will be right to do so. You may well say that in comprehensive education all are equal, so why shouldn't the working classes understand what is taught as well as the middle-class child? Actually the middle-class child doesn't really understand any of it either, for our whole teaching system is so unhealthy that really none of what is taught there is understood. And only some, specifically those who belong to the ruling classes, are rich enough to get to higher education, where these high schools and universities cast a shadow back on elementary education, so that these students then understand what they learned when they were younger. Those who have no chance to cast a shadow backwards on what they learned previously, will have no means of absorbing anything from the schooling they receive, a schooling that lives among us today as a kind of dreamed reality.

These things are typical of the grave nature of our times, of the situation we find ourselves in. Isn't it quite apparent, therefore, that only a new life of spirit, a new culture, can help us? Try for a moment to appraise things honestly in one or another field. Take art for instance, developments in the last few decades in the art world and in understanding of art. Try for a moment to form a picture in your mind of how people have been speaking about art, what artists themselves have been saying about how one ought to paint or sculpt and so forth, and what view critics then express about these painters and sculptors. If you try to trace all this and then describe it to the manual labourer who stands eight hours at his machine every day, and is supposed to listen to you lecture him on the subject, he will think it's garbage, meaningless. What is real to him is only that he sees from afar a life that the others enjoy, from which he is excluded— antisocially so—and which he cannot therefore perceive as being part of a life of human dignity. For him it is all only privileged luxury.

But let's look at this in detail, dear friends! It is not as if I want to condemn anything, I'm only characterizing. It's all understandable. But let's examine the shoots sprouting from this comfortable, middle-class order of society up to 1914. I myself witnessed this in the 1880s, when for instance the Viennese school was modelling itself on new departures in art that had begun in Paris. Its adherents composed endless verses, did all in their power to get dark rings round their eyes, wandered about in lofty thought on the streets and praised the merits of '*la décadence*'. They declared that they would only sleep in a room pervaded by the heady aroma of the tuberose. And drawing on all this refinement, they discussed the most elegant form for their verses. I am not condemning these phenomena—it expressed one aspect of humanity, in somewhat extreme form. But what issued from this ultimately could only appear as privileged luxury to a great number of people today. Inevitably it did not strike them, at least, as necessary to a humane existence. Everything ultimately depends on what pulses in human souls, and the way in which human souls can enter into life, how they can live and move there. What came to expression at that time was actually a social carcinoma, the outbreak of disease.

These things must teach us that reality will not allow us any longer to express ourselves in the old, outmoded ways, and that we must learn a new language. Isn't it palpably clear, my dear friends, that we must now seek something universally human. People will not immediately grasp the degree to which our building expresses this universally human quality, but that is what we have attempted to express with it. It should contain nothing that interests only the privileged classes, or that the proletarian cannot make head or tail of. Despite calling on people's highest spiritual nature, what we have attempted here is something absolutely universally human. Yes, it is imperfect in many ways, and there are still middle-class aspects to it, but overall and primarily what we have tried to do here is universally human. Its forms, albeit drawn from the spirit, are something comprehensible to any and every human being.

It can be understood from a living point of view. It is true that because people bring their own particular perspectives when they come here, we have to talk to them about the building in diverse ways. And yet it is possible nevertheless to show to the simplest, most primitive sensibility what is trying to speak from the forms or other aspects of our building. Similarly, in every field of life, efforts must be made to leave the old behind and speak a new language; to see how the old modes of thinking are what led us to catastrophe.

Look, people often regard modern socialism with horror, and compare it, say, with the spirit of the Sermon on the Mount, which teaches that the meek and poor in spirit can come to a new world order not through class conflict but through love. I am not making this up—these are things expressed by very well-known sermonisers. In recent weeks such things have been expressed countless times. Just a couple of days ago someone in Bern was saying[59] that we should return to the pure spirit of Christianity, to the spirit of the Sermon on the Mount, as opposed to that of modern class warfare. He went on to regret that the spirit of Christianity had so far been confined to people's private lives, and that it ought to be integrated into political life. Outer, public life, he thought, should be Christianized. People come and tell you about this and say, 'At last! Someone is speaking of the spirit, of how modern humanity can redeem itself from the pitfalls of materialism and return to the spirit of love.' But the truth, my dear friends, is that people have been saying such things for close on two thousand years, and it has never helped. They should recognize that we need a new language.

But today people often completely fail to notice the difference between the two languages. They simply do not recognize how radically different it is to propound a life of spirit, a spiritual culture, that seeks to engage fully and directly in the most material reality. This outlook is convinced that matter as such, matter alone, is no reality at all, but that matter should not be despised since spirit lives in all reality. And where only matter apparently exists, people are just failing to see the spirit. For this reason we must also be clear about the urgent need today to develop a spirit that really masters reality, that can immerse itself in material life, and does not only propose inner contemplation, finding the God within, developing the source of love. It is thought that this will enable us to find a way from the state of modern society to one where people have deep inner affinity with each other. But no. Today we have to find a spirit, a language, a Christianity that do not expound ethical and religious matters alone but that are so strong in spirit that the spirit becomes able to encompass the most prosaic and mundane of things; that through this spirit we can say what ought to happen to find the path, the path of healing, that leads us out of the cataclysms of capitalism, out of the indignity of seeing human beings only as a workforce, and so on.

While people have a sense of what is wrong with the social organism, what makes it sick, they cannot fathom the underlying problems. The harm done by money, in small ways and great, is generally recognized. On a small scale many see that they do not have money. The old serenity, which accepted how things were with a shrug of the shoulders, has come to an end. This was summed up in proverbs such as 'one man holds the purse but the other has the money'. People now reject such quietism. They observe the injuries of various kinds caused by the economic system, even if they don't get to travel abroad much any more. Yes, peace has been concluded but they cross borders less than they could during the war. Yet they see that a Mark is worth so much in another region, and so much less where they live. The currency question is connected with the whole money issue. So people notice that something is wrong with money, both on a large and a small scale, and that this relates to the most everyday human circumstances. And they ponder on how the harm done might be remedied a little. But they fail to see the need to move on from ordinary, external thoughts, closely connected to circumstances, to far deeper and more primary levels of thought.

Certain primary ideas underlie all human institutions. And when human life leads these institutions gradually ever further away from their originating ideas, these archetypes of thought withdraw into human interiority and become feelings and instincts, and express themselves in ways in which we can immediately recognize an archetypal character. The social demands that are surfacing today express the reaction of these primary thoughts to human circumstances in society. And people who model their ideas very closely on social circumstances today are the worst fantasists—for all the demands of the proletariat are in fact masked and concealed feelings rooted in primary thoughts. These primary ideas include the separation of spiritual life, the political life of the state and economic life as we have proposed it. It is toward this that people's instincts tend, and will not rest until some headway has been made in this direction. The grave crisis in which we live today shows how far we have grown distant from primary, originating ideas.

Everything else will be shallow quackery, even when dealing with the most external, most material issues. Take money for instance. Economics professors grandly ask what money is, and there is much debate about it. Is money a commodity or merely a token of value? Some think it's just one commodity among others and as such can be traded on the market like other goods; that it is a commodity with the convenience of avoiding various conflicts that you would otherwise have in a modern economy. Imagine you're a carpenter or joiner in a world without money. You have to eat. You need vegetables, cheese, butter. But as a carpenter you make tables and chairs. You take these to market and have to try to sell your wares, let's say trade a chair for sufficient food, or exchange a table for the clothes a tailor has made. What a fuss and bother this would be. Actually this is exactly what happens, really, masked only by the fact that we have a generally accepted commodity, money, which we can trade everything for and which can then be held until we need to trade it for different goods.

Thus it seems as if money were only an intermediate article, and many economists therefore think money is a commodity. But paper money only exists as a substitute for a commodity, backed up by gold. And countries have found it necessary to introduce the gold standard, gold currency, since the leading economic state today, England, has chosen gold as the sole value standard, trading standard, and the other countries had to follow suit. We now have a situation, therefore, in which this intermediate commodity exists, and the carpenter doesn't have to carry his tables to market but can sell them to anyone who wants them, getting money in exchange, with which he can then buy his cheese and vegetables.

But others say that the nature of money is quite different, since it doesn't matter at all—and practice has to some extent confirmed this—whether we really own the little piece of gold that is worth so and so much in relation to other goods, or whether it doesn't exist at all but is instead just some kind of substitute bearing the stamp of a particular value. Our modern paper money bears this value stamp, indicating what it is worth. And there are economists today who think it is irrelevant whether or not the gold corresponding in value to these paper tokens is actually there in the bank. As you may know, there are also countries that only have paper currency and no gold in the bank to back it up. Under present circumstances they too can run their economies in this way.

At least you can see from this—and in our domain we must found our views on a purely human perspective—that there are clever people today who regard money as a commodity and other clever people who think it is just a stamp, a token. So what is it actually? Under present conditions it is both. It is important to recognize that, as conditions are today, it is both at once: that on the one hand, particularly in international trading, money often has the character of a commodity only, for the rest is all credit transfers. What can seriously be regarded as the underwriting of value is trading of gold between different countries. Everything else relies on trust so that, when a certain amount of paper money or bills of draft or suchlike is supplied from one country to another, the state that furnishes it really possesses the gold that backs it; and that in other words the commodity exists, the commodity gold, which is then treated like any other commodity. You give a trader credit, don't you, irrespective of whether he is selling gold or fish or something else, as long as he has some kind of real asset as financial cover or backing. Thus on the international market especially, money is a commodity.

But the state has got mixed up in this, gradually turning money into something attributed a value, something with only token value. The one interacts with the other, and the harm done here is due to this. The only feasible remedy is to shift the whole administration of money over to what we have called the third sphere of the healthy social organism, the economic organism, releasing and detaching all finance administration from the political organism. And then money will become a commodity and will have to have its commodity value on the commodity market. This would get rid of that peculiar dependency that exists today, which represents an out-of-kilter relationship between currency values and wages. The odd thing today is that currency values fall when wages rise, so that however much you increase the worker's wages he gains no benefit from this since he can't buy any more with his money than he could before on his low wages. If wages increase, and the price of food keeps pace with these increases, or in other words currency values become quite different, all the other conditions will make no difference. The only remedy here is to remove administration of this economic asset too, of money, from the political state, so that the money there is can be administered by the third sphere, the economic sphere of the healthy social organism, so as to create true comparisons of value between one thing and another.

Fundamentally resolving society into these three spheres leads at the same time to the solving of such specific problems and the restoration of healthy conditions. This is why we need to return to core, primary ideas today if we are to have any hope of developing healthy ideas for the social organism. Modern governments are asking what to do about the chaotic nature of currency values. The only answer to this question is this: for heaven's sake leave it all alone if you are political administrators, and cede the administration of currency and money to the economic organism. Only there can healthy foundations be created for these matters. We really must return to what makes things healthy today. Before the devastating war broke out, we saw the curious fact—due to an international situation unaffected by state taxation levies within countries themselves—that in the international arena economic life necessarily arose by virtue of and through itself. This held true in the international arena, but not within countries themselves since there the state extended its structures over economic life. This gave rise to conflicts which can only be eradicated again if we really endeavour to establish threefolding. Then the realities at work in one sphere of the social organism will invariably correct the realities in another, if they need to be corrected. There is no other way forward today than to return to primary ideas, to this practical tripartite structure of spiritual and cultural life, economic life, political life. Only those actually involved in one of these spheres will be able to solve the issues that need solving, from one or another perspective. Only when economic activity is conducted by one sphere, democratic rights are administered in another, including the passing of legislation, and in the third all cultural and spiritual matters are regulated, can we create a healthier social organism. Just as the three spheres work together in the human organism—the head system with the cardiovascular system, and with the metabolic system—so the three spheres work naturally together also in the healthy social organism. One sphere interacts with the other. Just as you can get a headache resulting from a stomach problem—because the stomach no longer properly supplies the head—even though the three systems are separate, so in the social organism too, if it is really healthy, one sphere interacts with the other—the economic sphere, say, with the rights sphere, and with the cultural sphere. They interact properly precisely when each is relatively self-contained and autonomous. But this proper and untroubled interaction can only be established if the three spheres are independent from each other, and each is governed and regulated according to its own laws.

How, for instance, does spiritual, cultural life and activity interact with economic life? What aspect of the spirit is rightly present in economic life? Do you know? I'll tell you: capital. Capital is the spirit of economic life. And a great amount of harm existing in our day arises from the fact that the administration of capital, its fertilization and fruitfulness as it were, is withdrawn from the life of spirit. It is important that, in the healthy social organism, the relationship between, let's say, the manual worker and the person or group that organizes this work with the aid of capital, is seen as one of mutual trust only, founded on reciprocal understanding, in the same way, say, that we can have a free choice of school for our children. In the healthy social organism, the employer or entrepreneur can no longer live in a world apart from the employee. Today the labourer operates his machine or stands at his conveyor belt, and is involved in nothing more than these operations. And only outside the factory gates is he free to follow other pursuits. The employer in turn has his own life and circles—I described them to you before—which may involve various forms of decadent pursuit. The employer pursues cultural life that is separate and distinct from the rest of society. Yet we urgently need a kind of spiritual, cultural life that does not divide manual workers from mental workers, and then capitalism will have a social foundation: not of a kind suggested by modern fantasists, but one that makes it possible for each individual worker to be connected culturally with all those who organize his work and who in turn conduct the product of his work back into the social organism or even into the whole world.

Just as important as the worker's labour is that business matters are discussed at regular meetings between the employer and employee, so that the latter continually has an overview of what is happening. This is something we must endeavour to establish for the future. The employer should be required at any moment to tell the employee exactly what is happening, and discuss all its details with him, so that the factory or company is embedded in a shared culture. That's the important thing. Only then is it possible to establish the kind of relationship which will enable the worker to say, 'Yes, he is as necessary as I am, for without him my labour would get nowhere in the social organism. He directs my work to the right place.' And likewise the employer will have to actually do this, and accord the worker what is due him, for everything will be transparent.

Here you see, dear friends, how the life of spirit must play into the workings of capitalism. Anything else is just so much bluster, just fantasy. A healthy relationship between work and capital cannot be established by some kind of social bureaucracy but only through a shared culture in which someone who has the individual gifts and capacities to do so in this field, that is to work as a capitalist, can also be really productive, can make his individual skills fruitful for the healthy social organism, in the process eliciting the free understanding of the manual labourer. Thus understanding can arise for initiatives driven by individual capacities, for in the free life of spirit these will be intrinsically socially beneficial. They only have an antisocial tendency today because we are caught up in unnatural conditions. Socialization must be founded on the free initiative of individual capacities and on the free understanding that is brought to bear on what these capacities achieve. Nothing else will work. Anything else is charlatanism. It ought to be possible to see the truth of what I say here simply by observing the symptoms apparent in the social organism.

My dear friends, consider for a moment that there are things in the world about which people can, and do, hold extremely diverse views. Whereas anyone will tell you that a loaf of bread will feed someone when he's hungry, and no one will dispute this, a worldview is quite another matter: some will consider it true, others false. And however true it may be, it will get nowhere because of this. We can argue about such matters in the realm of culture, things of the spirit, but there is no dispute about the realities of economic life. Why is this? It is because the spirit has become ideology, no longer working as a reality but only as a secondary adjunct to economic life and political life. If founded on itself, it becomes necessary for this sphere to reveal its own reality to the world; and then reality will simply radiate from it. But then of course it will not merely figure in the idle loquaciousness of moral sermonizers, not simply figure in the speeches of those who tell us we should be good Christians and so on, as they vaunt all kinds of virtues but stop short before material realities. A bridge must be built between this abstract form of the spirit and the spirit that is really worthy of the name: which works for instance within capital, for it is capital that organizes labour. But this organizing activity must really be governed and administered by the spiritual sphere.

So on the one hand, in practical terms, financial administration must be left to economic life, while on the other hand work organized by capital should be governed by the life of spirit. And here you see the cooperative interaction of things that outwardly appear to be one, for of course capital is represented in the factory in monetary terms. But the relationship between employee and employer, this whole relationship of trust, the fact in particular that an employer or entrepreneur operates in a particular place, is organization issuing from the sphere of spirit, whereas the value of a particular commodity in monetary terms is organized in economic life; and these things flow together in the same way that in the human organism the outcome, or yield, of each of the three systems flows together to maintain the health of the organism.

Thus you can enter into tangible realities, the most mundane circumstances of life; and you will see that what we have flagged up here are really primary ideas, archetypes that must sustain the healing of the social organism.

LECTURE 7

DORNACH, 15 MARCH 1919

If you attentively examine human history you will find a certain theme running through it: a characteristic reluctance to focus thoughts on what is being asked by the clearly audible realities unfolding in the world. In general people are disinclined to consider ideas that do not run on well-worn tracks. But perhaps there has never been a time when this was so apparent—when people were so averse to entertaining ideas they had never previously considered. There's an underlying phenomenon running through history which has come to the fore today particularly. I have spoken a good deal about how this manifested several years back. If you think back to the spring and early summer of 1914, you could compile a fine collection of speeches by European statesmen, all with a similar theme. Foreign Secretary Jagow,[60] for instance, gave a speech in the German parliament to the effect that efforts made by European governments have succeeded in creating good relationships between the great powers in Europe, and peace is therefore assured for long ages to come. The same thought, with slight variations, was expressed by all these 'pragmatists' as they liked to think of themselves. Well, that was back then. And only a few weeks later the conflagration erupted, culminating in the present disaster. What are we now witnessing in the stated aims and measures proposed by people who belong so thoroughly to their time? In the last few days I have heard various things figuring in the 'League of Nations Conference' in Bern.[61] Despite the variety of themes that were raised there, everything said about the shape of things to come was more or less of like kind with the speeches made by European statesmen in the spring and early summer of 1914. These people think along well-worn tracks, and say the same things they have always been accustomed to saying. Really they have learned nothing, and I mean nothing, of the lessons of the past four-and-a-half years which have been audibly speaking to us from the depths of world existence.

This is something that a spiritual scientist, particularly, must attend to very keenly. A desolation has spread across large swathes of the European continent. Despite the many variations of message, it seems highly typical, merely something pushed to an extreme, if people are talking of a worldview and a movement which, though it rises from subterranean depths of a kind calamitous for our era, will have great prospects of making strong headway: of securing great conquests simply because of the indifference, the lack of interest amongst the peoples of Europe. When I was very young—a long time ago now—our religion books sought to impress upon us children the nature of Christ Jesus by stating the following: he was, said these books, either a hypocrite, a fool or what he himself stated, the son of the living God. And since the assumption that he was either of the first two could not be countenanced, the only option was to believe that what he said was true—that he was indeed the son of the living God. Well, this old argument, which I read in my religion books as a child, I heard again very recently in a talk that followed the League of Nations Conference in Bern. The talk was given by Professor Ude of Graz University.[62] And he said this: Jesus was either a hypocrite or a fool, or he was what he himself said, the son of the living God. 'And since,' this professor exclaimed, 'you will not dare to call Christ a hypocrite or a fool, he can only have been what he said of himself, the son of the living God!' He hurled these words into the audience with Jesuitical vehemence. And there can have been very few there who asked themselves the only meaningful question in response to such an utterance: how has this little saying, repeated to the faithful for centuries, helped prevent the ruin and calamity that has broken over our heads? Is there no feeling and awareness of the pointlessness of shouting such things into a crowd, and continuing to shout them, after the world catastrophe we have witnessed and everything contributing to it that has proven so palpably fruitless? I attended another talk, too, by the same professor, on the social question. And he did not refer even once in the whole talk to any possible remedy. From beginning to end his lecture was just a kind of condemnation of various malpractices and bad habits which do—certainly—exist today. And yet here too nothing has been learned from the sad events of the last four-and-a-half years.

I cite this example, rather than others, because Professor Ude's talks were by far the best of those given in Bern by many different figures. At least they were rooted in a worldview, albeit one which, widely propounded today, will inevitably prove dangerous. The other talks testified to an inability on the part of the speakers to even raise themselves to some kind of worldview or outlook on life. People's thinking has become dull and short-sighted, and we must keep stressing this fact. They are unable to penetrate realities. They live in illusions, on the surface of things. It is hard to see how these speakers are actually contributing to the reshaping of the world so much needed today.

My dear friends, we must keep reminding ourselves that over the past four centuries European humanity, with its American offspring, has developed a form of thinking that can only grasp the dead and lifeless realm. We have come up with a thinking completely oriented to mathematics and technology. We have become incapable of directing our thoughts to what lives in the natural world. We only understand what is dead. The knowledge we can express about the organism in our official, mainstream science only applies to the dead organism and is gained from a study of the corpse. And yet this same thinking, which has become customary, is now applied to the social organism as well. But this means only that a great proportion of humanity has become unable to form thoughts about the living social organism at all. At best they find it very difficult to form such thoughts, much preferring the ease of reciting *ad infinitum* what has been drummed into them for centuries, like a catechism: thoughts that run on well-worn tracks, or otherwise the offspring of these thoughts now applied to the corpse of the living organism. But what is needed today, actually, is an understanding of the living social organism.

Let's take something specific. Modern socialist thought, as I have described in the past in all its aspects, rails extensively against capitalism. Socialism demands that all private capital be socialized, or in other words transferred to the means of production. The 'National Assembly' in Weimar, as I believe it is called, has discussed this socialization extensively. But the very way in which people discuss capitalism today originates in the dead thinking of recent centuries, which has become a decisive aspect of the purely scientific, materialistic worldview. What we find here, my dear friends, is that capitalism has basically indeed become a terrible oppressor of the population at large. It will be hard to find many objections to everything that has been said, and goes on being said, by the proletarian movement against the oppressive nature of capitalism, in terms of human rights and the economy. But what conclusion do socialist thinkers draw from this undeniable fact? They say that capitalism must therefore be abolished: it is after all oppressive, something dire; it has proven itself to be a scourge of modern humanity and so must be abolished. What could be more comprehensible, what could seem more instrumental for campaigning purposes—though this has now led to dire unrest throughout Europe—than this demand for the abolition of capitalism? But for anyone who does not resort solely to the dead thinking of the past four centuries, and is instead able to invoke the living thinking that we need above all for our science of the spirit, this idea of abolishing capitalism—because it is a scourge, an oppressor of humanity—is as logical as to say the following: we continually breathe in oxygen and breathe out dead carbon dioxide; oxygen is transformed in us into carbon dioxide, so why even bother breathing it in? It just becomes death-delivering poison in us. And yet to live we *have* to breathe it in. The living processes of the animal and human organism are inconceivable without breathing in oxygen. In the same way, the life of society is inconceivable without the continual creation of capital, especially today without the continual development of the means of production, and in reality this is, basically, capital. There is no social organism that would not have to rely on the collaboration of individual human skills and capacities. If an understanding of the real needs of the social organism were to become widespread, the worker would recognize the need to trust in the director of an enterprise; would see that if the company director did not run the company, he, the worker, could not perform his work. That is entirely self-evident. But when there are company directors, it necessarily follows that capital accumulates. There simply is no way to avoid the accumulation of capital. So however well-meaning it might be to ask how capital can be abolished, the question is tantamount to asking how we could destroy the social organism altogether, how we might kill it off.

It is perfectly apparent to anyone with any understanding of these things that capital accumulates in even the most sane and reasonable social order, and it is equally apparent that it is pointless to wonder how to prevent this, how to eradicate it. And yet people seem to find it too difficult to face this fact squarely. They'd rather not entertain such an idea. They want their thinking to be easy. Yet the times we live in will not allow us to make things easy for ourselves in this way. What people always forget is that all life is in growth and flux, that time is an element we need as we try to understand life; that living things are not fixed and constant but always changing. It is not difficult to recognize this—the part played by time in our understanding of life. After all, the human organism is alive. Consider the human organism—in fact *your own* organism—at about half past one in the afternoon. You're all hard-working people who don't hang about too long in the cafeteria, and when you emerge from the cafeteria after lunch, then all being well you're not hungry for a while. Your organism is, I'm quite sure, a tangible, human organism. And so, as you define it at about quarter to two in the afternoon, as you emerge from the cafeteria, it is a living being without hunger.

But at half past twelve, when you were going into the cafeteria, all of you were hungry; and so you might define the human organism at that point as one that feels hunger. Of course you are considering specific, actual life at two different moments in time, and you find that what this organism needs to thrive at these two different moments are opposing states that must be created in your organism: the first is a process necessary for the opposite to occur. This holds true both for natural organisms and social ones too. In the living social realm we can never prevent capital arising as a self-evident phenomenon that accompanies the work of individual human capacities, as the development of property, of private property. If someone directs a branch of production, and quite justifiably shares the yield of what is produced with the manual labourers who make it, the social organism simply could not survive without capital as an accompanying phenomenon: capital owned by the individual just as he owns what he needs for his own use, and what he produces which he then trades or exchanges to meet his own needs.

Just as little as we could prohibit the eating of food because it is a nuisance to get hungry again after eating, so it is impossible to try to prevent capital being created at a particular time. Instead we should think only about how this capital must be transformed in turn at a different moment in time, what should become of it. Unless you want to undermine the sustainability of the social organism, it is impossible to try to prevent the creation of capital. All you can try to do is assure that the capital which is created does not become harmful within the healthy social organism.

It is only possible to realize this requirement, which is necessary for the healing of the social organism, in the *threefold* social organism; for only there—as in the natural human organism—can one sphere work in a contrary way to the other. It lies in an individual's interests that a sphere exists in the social organism in which individual human abilities come to expression; but equally it lies in everyone's interests that these individual human capacities do not, over time, transform in a way that becomes harmful to the organism. In the economic cycle, capital will always be created. If you leave this capital circulating within the economic cycle, it leads to unlimited accumulation of wealth. You cannot allow the capital accumulating as a result of individual human abilities to remain an economic asset, but must, rather, transfer it into the rights sphere. You see, the moment a person obtains more for what he himself alone produces, or produces in common with others, than what he spends or consumes, his asset is truly no longer a commodity, any more than human labour can be one. Ownership of an asset is a right. Ownership in fact is nothing other than an exclusive right to use something—let's say land or property—and to exclude all others from holding such a right to it. No other definition of ownership is of use in understanding the social organism. And this means that the moment someone acquires ownership of something, this ownership is something that must be administered within the purely political state, within the rights sphere. But the state itself must not acquire it, for otherwise it becomes an economic player. Its role is only to transfer it to the spiritual organism where people's individual abilities are administered. What I am describing only happens today with goods regarded as being the most 'paltry' in economic value. For these it does happen, but not for valuable goods.

If someone creates a spiritual product—let's say a major poem, an important work as a writer or an artist—he can bequeath the yield of this work to his descendants for a period of thirty years. After that it is released from copyright and no longer passes to his descendants but to all humanity. Thirty years after the death of a writer, you can freely reprint his works.[63] A really healthy idea underlies this: the idea that we owe what we posses as our individual gifts to all of society. Just as little as we could learn to speak human language on an isolated island, with no human company, so we can only develop our individual gifts within society. These gifts are founded of course on our own karma but they have to be developed through society and so in a sense we owe them to society. They must return to society again; we only have custodianship of them for a certain period, for it is better for the social organism that we do hold this custodianship. This is because we ourselves are most intimate with what we have produced, and so can manage it best. These 'paltry' values, as modern humanity sees them, are the spiritual ones, and so in a sense they are evaluated in social terms, and governed by the idea of time.

I have been told that some of my audience at a recent lecture in Bern,[64] capitalists apparently, were livid when I asked why a law couldn't be passed obliging the owners of capital, a certain number of years after their death, to relinquish their capital to the free governance of a body, a spiritual-cultural organization, in the spiritual sphere of the social organism. There are of course many different ways of establishing a specific law. But people are outraged if you propose returning to the legal practice of ancient Hebrew times, when the distribution of goods was reallocated after a certain period. And what is the outcome of their outrage? That over the last four-and-a-half years humankind has killed ten million people and made eighteen million into cripples, and is now embarking on more such devastation. It is essential today to reflect on these things. It really does matter whether or not we invoke the idea of time when studying the social organism. People conceive of society in entirely atemporal terms when they say that this or that should happen with capital as it originates, in its *status nascens*. Yes, we must let capital emerge and must let those who gave rise to it administer it for a while; but then we must be able to allow it to return again into the true commonality of humankind through a healthily functioning, that is threefold, social organism.

You can't ask why a single social organism could not accomplish all this too. People believe this but to do so takes very poor account of the human psyche. We have to reckon with the human soul. Consider what happens if a judge is trying the case of a near or distant relative. He will have his personal feelings about this relative, but in issuing his judgement he will not be guided by these feelings but by the law, of course. His judgement will come from a different source. If you think through the psychology of this you can see the need for people to judge from three different sources, and administer from three different directions, what flows together in the social organism. Our era is asking us to engage with such things, for it is the age of the consciousness soul. And this consciousness-soul era needs people to base their actions on the guiding impulse of clear and specific ideas.

Nowadays many urge that we should relinquish reason and abstract thinking—the only kind of thinking they know about—and instead judge things more intuitively and, especially in matters relating to interpersonal relations, maintain a certain faith. They think that thinking is really only the preserve of science and academe. This is a questionable stance because it is precisely in our era that people have developed faculties of extreme abstract thinking. They want to entertain only the most linear concepts and, having established them, they cling to them with huge tenacity. This abstract thinking is primarily of a kind that prioritizes only the human head, a thinking most of all bound to the physical organ of the head. Formerly, when atavistic clairvoyance still existed, this thinking faculty was imbued by a spiritually oriented thinking rising from the rest of the human organism. The time of atavistic clairvoyance is past. And now people must elevate themselves consciously and intentionally to imaginations, must consciously encompass the life of spirit; if they do not, people's thoughts will remain empty.

As you know from our recent reflections, the head we bear on our shoulders today is in fact the rest of the organism, apart from the head, that belonged to us during our last incarnation.[65] I have often spoken of this. The formative forces of the head—naturally not its physical substance—whose roundness is created in the image of the cosmos, pass over into the cosmos. The forces that accompany our life between death and rebirth, and in the next incarnation become our head, to be joined by the new organism from the mother's body, fertilized by the father, are those of the rest of the body in our last incarnation. At death we lose our head, one may say, in so far as its forces are spent, and we transform the forces of the rest of our organism into the head of our next incarnation. The great mass of modern mankind, in their past incarnation, despised this earthly vale of tears as it was regarded in Christianity. This disdain is a feeling, connected with the whole body, not bound to the head. And as they reincarnate today, what in their last life was a seemingly very lofty

Christian sentiment, develops the organ of the head and in doing so is transformed into its opposite, becoming a yearning for matter, a longing for material life. Humanity today has come to a turning point in evolution where, it has to be said, very little indeed has entered their head from their former incarnation. And precisely for this reason it is vital that something new must enter human beings, a revelation of the present, something newly revealed to people from the world of spirit. It is no longer possible today merely to cite the Gospels. Instead we must hearken to what is being said spiritually to us as humanity. The Catholic Church, for example, also participates in dead thinking of a kind unable to grasp the living organism. In Bern again, Catholic speakers did not weary of proclaiming Christ as the son of the living God. But my dear friends, what use is this if we encompass Christ only with dead thinking, that is, if he becomes only a dead ideal in our thoughts? Rather than invoking Christ, the son of the living God, what we need today is to invoke Christ, the *living* son of God—in other words, the Christ who is now alive and working to bring humanity new revelations.

It is in this sense that spiritual science, specifically, seeks to find the impulse of all our thinking in the new revelation coming directly from spiritual worlds. But this would give people thoughts capable of fathoming reality. And in many respects these thoughts would be the very opposite of those that dominate minds today. People today want to cling to the cleverest thoughts which are, however, as far removed as possible from reality. Once they possess such a thought, they cling to it in an extraordinary manner, not noticing the realities that actually hold sway, and in some circumstances modify thinking. Let me give you a striking instance of this.

Like the statesmen who spoke of world peace in the spring and summer of 1914, the various 'international' speakers in Bern spoke of the planned League[66] of Nations. As you know, the idea of this League of Nations springs from the head of Woodrow Wilson. In his speech in January 1917, Wilson formulated this idea. He proposed it as something we should aspire to, so as to avoid in future further dire catastrophes such as those into which we have been driven in modern times. He described this League of Nations as an absolute necessity, at the same time saying that its realization will depend on a specific condition, without which such a League cannot be established. This prerequisite was that the war should end without any side being victorious, for a League of Nations could never be realized, he said, if a decisive victory was gained by one side at the expense of a decisive defeat for the other.

Yes, that was the condition which Wilson said was critical to the founding of a League of Nations. And what has now come about is the precise opposite of Wilson's requirement. Yet the hypothetical league which Wilson described in January 1917 is now going to be founded despite this. This is a prime example of being very far removed from reality in your thoughts, of clinging to an idea without any means of penetrating or engaging with reality, an inability to encompass this reality in your thinking. Yet that is the most essential thing today. People fail to see that they must not stop short in their thoughts but must use them to perceive and fathom realities.

One well-meaning person in Bern was the pacifist Schücking.[67] People were talking about this League of Nations and how its institutions would work. Curiously, it was being said that just as separate countries have parliaments, so we should aspire to an overriding supranational parliament. To the objection that the various nations were independent entities, and would therefore not submit to a unified, centralized leadership at a supranational level, Schücking replied that the example of the National Assembly in Weimar showed this was possible. All the little territorial principalities were, he said, likewise independent entities, but they could see the usefulness of an encompassing whole. It is easy to see why people wedded to abstractions might think this: what could be more self-evident than seeing the many small principalities joined together in the National Assembly as an example of something that could be realized on a larger scale with a superstate? But anyone who thinks in real, specific terms will go on to ask how this became possible in Weimar. It came about through the German Revolution! Otherwise it would have been unthinkable. A supranational parliament modelled on the Weimar National Assembly could only come about after a world revolution! This is thinking that connects with realities, does not sunder itself from them and would, if it did, feel itself to be sick and ailing.

It is so difficult to make people realize that we need a new thinking, a truly new kind of reality-friendly thinking, and that the healing of our condition will depend on people inclining toward this reality-friendly thinking. But thinking with no interest in the world of spirit cannot fathom reality, for this world of spirit lives in all reality. Those who wish to know nothing about the world of spirit are least able to fathom reality, and will be still less able to in future. Whether or not humanity turns to spiritual-scientific knowledge is therefore one of the primary questions today for the healing of our modern world. This has to be the foundation—and could be, can easily be. It is superficial tittle-tattle to keep saying it is so hard to introduce this science of the spirit into the real world, that people reject it. Please don't say such things! All that is needed is to abolish state supervision of universities, secondary schools, primary schools, and in ten years spiritual science, or at least its necessary and primary foundations, will have replaced our modern, soul-ruining and soul-deadening academe. What could already today spring from the emancipated third of the healthy social organism, from the spiritual, cultural sphere, will look very different from what has been superintended by the state, which seeks only to educate its priests to propound a theology acceptable to the state, to educate its jurists as state jurists, not to mention its doctors. The state suppresses any form of medicine not confined within state boundaries, at all costs dismissing as ridiculous a knowledge that aims to heal people wherever they are in the world.

As I have often said, socialist thinking regards all spiritual, cultural life as ideology. What is the deeper reason for this? Why is all culture, in the thinking of the proletarian masses, seen as an ideology? Well, it is because all knowledge is supposed to be underpinned by something external, by the political state, since it is only the shadow of this political state. It *is* indeed ideology. For spiritual, cultural life not to be ideology it must continually demonstrate its reality through its own powers, that is, it must be emancipated and self-founded. Spiritual life must continually demonstrate its reality, must not have an outer crutch. Only a life of spirit and culture without a crutch, founded only on human capacities and gifts, only self-administering, will be able also to send its currents into capitalism in a healthy way. Capitalist governance is in fact nothing other than one effected by human capacities. If you make spiritual, cultural life healthy at its core, it becomes healthy too where it flows into capitalism and governs economic life.

Thus are things connected, in a context we must come to understand. My dear friends, we must avoid all the reality-estranged thinking of those wedded to abstraction, which we meet at every turn and which has led to our current parlous circumstances. People do not yet recognize this.

Nowadays they ask what form the world state should have, thinking that it should be simply modelled on what the state as they know it has been and done so far. But would it not be much wiser to ask what this state should refrain from doing? The states in Europe brought about the catastrophic war, and it is much more self-evident to ask what they should stop doing. They should stop involving themselves in the life of the spirit, they should stop acting as entrepreneurs. They should confine themselves to the political domain alone. We cannot ask how a League of Nations should be founded and base this on what states have done hitherto or should have done. It is better and more topical today to ask what they should refrain from doing.

As yet people are still disinclined to really engage with such things. But the fate of humanity today will depend on whether they do engage with them or not. Today was by way of introduction to these themes, and tomorrow I will speak further about them.

Lecture 8

DORNACH, 16 MARCH 1919

One instance of the many signs that modern thinking is far removed from reality is, as I said yesterday, that in the circles concerned with founding a League of Nations no one considers how—in the form in which the idea sprang from the head of Woodrow Wilson—it was originally proposed as something that would only work if neither side in the conflict could claim victory. I want to read you the speech where he set out these preconditions for the League of Nations on 22 January 1917. Wilson says:

> The statesmen of both of the groups of nations now arrayed against one another have said, in terms that could not be misinterpreted, that it was no part of the purpose they had in mind to crush their antagonists. But the implications of these assurances may not be equally clear to all—may not be the same on both sides of the water. I think it will be serviceable if I attempt to set forth what we understand them to be.
>
> They imply, first of all, that it must be a peace without victory. It is not pleasant to say this. I beg that I may be permitted to put my own interpretation upon it and that it may be understood that no other interpretation was in my thought.
>
> I am seeking only to face realities and to face them without soft concealments. Victory would mean peace forced upon the loser, a victor's terms imposed upon the vanquished. It would

be accepted in humiliation, under duress, at an intolerable sacrifice, and would leave a sting, a resentment, a bitter memory upon which terms of peace would rest, not permanently, but only as upon quicksand.

Only a peace between equals can last. Only a peace the very principle of which is equality and a common participation in a common benefit. The right state of mind, the right feeling between nations, is as necessary for a lasting peace as is the just settlement of vexed questions of territory or of racial and national allegiance.

This was the condition asserted as necessary for a League of Nations. And if our thinking is clear, dear friends, we must conclude that the moment the secured peace does not fulfil this condition, but enshrines the victory of one side, any talk of a League of Nations must be relinquished since it would have no chance of thriving. Yet that is not what happened. People's thinking does not accord with reality: they think in abstract terms, and allow thoughts to trundle on mechanically, quite irrespective of whether the original conception underlying them still applies or not.

This is just one striking example of a thinking that has led the world into such grave misfortune. And conditions will certainly not improve in a way wholesome for humanity unless this reality-estranged thinking gives way to one capable of penetrating and fathoming reality. This applies not only to great geopolitical affairs but also to the everyday life of each individual. In fact the small affairs of individuals have a close connection with the largest concerns of humankind. We have to keep inwardly seeking for what might bring about the real change that is necessary in our time.

We know of course that to take up the science of the spirit involves more than acquiring a certain conviction about supersensible worlds. That is the *content*. But someone who fully integrates into his thinking what can be justifiably communicated today about supersensible worlds, as spiritual revelations fitting for our time, must cultivate not only content, but a different mode and manner of thinking: his thinking must gradually reconfigure itself so that he can gain a sense of, and interest for, what is truly occurring in the world. As well as acknowledging truths through the science of the spirit, we must also transform our manner of thinking. And this will lead us to ask still more keenly why there is such resistance to spiritual science in the world today.

Yesterday I pointed out that everything we might say about this resistance must at the same time be related to all that could arise through the influence of the threefold social organism. I said yesterday that if we were really to stand up effectively for the autonomous, self-founded position of the life of spirit, independent from the economic cycle and the political life of the state, then spiritual science would gain currency and acceptance relatively quickly. But we can ask a still deeper question: Why are people today so disinclined to recognize the inevitable result of emancipating the life of spirit and culture by placing it on its own, autonomous footing? In fact this is because, in the modern era, this life of spirit and culture has acquired a certain form that itself prevents people from directing their gaze toward the world of spirit. One might even say that the dismal events of our time could be seen as a kind of punishment meted out to humanity for its failure to perceive the real nature of the life of spirit—a failure of insight that has arisen in modern times. My dear friends, it is important to recognize the existential necessity in future of leading human thoughts in a social direction. The facts themselves teach us this, and to bury one's head in the sand is foolish in the extreme. On the other hand, as will be apparent from various accounts I have given you, any kind of socialism devoid of simultaneous spiritualization will, for profound and deep-seated reasons, not bring salvation but disaster to humanity. One basis for acknowledging this can be found by carefully studying socialist thinking and its emergence from the rest of modern thinking.

I have already hinted at what is at work here, and today we will summarize some of these allusions. I said that minds such as Fichte testify to something which, when they apply their thinking to the social realm, leads to a view very similar in nature to what we encounter, for instance, in Bolshevism today. I said that Johann Gottlieb Fichte would have been a real Bolshevik! Of course, he also had sufficient spirituality to ensure that the Bolshevik ideas he published in *The Closed Commercial State* posed no danger for humanity. But nowadays people have so little inclination to engage with the real content of things that they do not notice the authentically Bolshevik nature of Fichte in this book of his.

Hegel offers us a thinking especially characteristic of modern times. And Karl Marx in turn, as I said, based his thinking on Hegel, albeit in a highly curious manner. Now I want to take this opportunity of speaking about the particular quality of Hegelian thinking, even if this will seemingly—and only seemingly—lead us into rarefied heights of abstraction. Commentators on Hegel in the turmoil of the past four-and-a-half years have said much about him that is extremely inaccurate. It seems fitting to offer redress now in the form of an objective appraisal of his intentions.

Let us consider how Hegel thought about the world, his efforts to fathom how world secrets are revealed to mankind. Hegel's comments on the essential nature of the world are often easy to survey, most clearly of all in his *Encyclopaedia of the Philosophical Sciences*. Let us examine, in a popular, accessible form, what worldview Hegel is expressing here. It can be subdivided into three parts.

The first part is what he calls 'logic'. For Hegel this does not refer to the art of subjective human thinking but he regards it instead as the sum of all the ideas that are active in the world itself. You see, Hegel does not regard ideas simply as a sort of phantom in human heads—this, he thinks, is only our view or perception of the idea. For Hegel, ideas are in a sense forces, powers at work within things themselves. The ideas that have not yet come to creative expression in nature, or have not yet been mirrored within human beings, and thus been perceived and recognized, are ideas in themselves, which work in the world. I realize of course that this won't make a lot of sense to you. But people have been saying for a long time that Hegel makes little sense to them; and this is because they cannot imagine a pure tissue of ideas existing somewhere in the world. Hegel regards this pure tissue or weft of ideas as being God before the creation of the world. And thus he sees God as a sum, or better, an organism of ideas, in the form in which they existed before the natural world arose, and before, in turn, the human being developed from natural foundations. This is how Hegel seeks to present ideas in pure logic. This is God before the world was created. In other words, God before the world's creation is pure logic.

Now one could say that it would be very useful for human culture if someone were to establish all the originating ideas in existence, irrespective of whether these were ideas of a living God or just a kind of spider's web of ideas hovering somewhere in the air—which would not have existed yet either. This would be useful for the human soul. But if you study this pure logic of Hegel's you find nothing more—and this is why so few people bother to study him—than a further tissue of ideas. He starts with the flimsiest concept, that of pure being, from there ascending to non-being, then to existence, and so on. You are therefore being asked to posit the sum of all ideas that the human being formulates about the world, but which he rarely reflects upon since he finds this too boring, from pure existence through to the purposeful development and structure of the organism; and to do so quite irrespective of any outer world. In this way you obtain a sum of ideas, but only abstract ideas. And our living feeling will naturally react to this sum or organism of abstract ideas. Let's assume someone says that it is a pantheistic preconception on Hegel's part to assume ideas in themselves pre-exist; to assume a God existed before the creation of the world, and that he had these particular ideas, and created the world according to them. What would you say about the presumption of asserting this inner life of God, this picture of the reason and inner life of a God who possessed nothing but Hegelian ideas and was thus always cogitating on what lives between pure being and purposeful organisms, who possessed nothing but ideas in their most extreme, abstract form? You would fail to comprehend how a God could be so impoverished as only to think these abstract ideas in his divine reason. And yet for Hegel, the sum of these abstract ideas is God himself, not only divine reason, but the very nature of God before the world was created. This is the important thing: that Hegel in reality does not get beyond abstract ideas, instead regarding these as the essence of divine being.

Then he proceeds to a second element, which is nature. Here again I could outline and define for you how Hegel proceeds from the idea, that is, from God before the creation of the world, to nature. But this again would not be very illuminating for you if you adhere to modern habits of thought. According to Hegel, logic contains the idea in its intrinsic being, the idea in itself. The natural world contains the idea in its externalization, outside of its intrinsic being. So what you see around you as nature is also idea, and is really nothing other than what logic contains, but just in this other form of extrapolation. And then Hegel traces nature through from mere mechanistics to an account of biological, botanical, animal conditions. That is, he seeks to demonstrate the existence of ideas within the whole scope of nature as we know it—the idea in light, in heat, in other forces, in gravity and so on.

Hegel recompenses any reader who can make head or tail of his abstractions with a vivid pictorial quality peculiar to him. This pictorial clarity in Hegel sometimes endangers our understanding of his actual intentions. I once tried to defend Hegel to a friend of mine, a professor of philosophy. I think it more useful to defend whatever is positive in anything than to insist always on one's own opinion and criticize everything else to death. I always defend anything good—part of the positivism of spiritual science. But in this instance my defence of Hegel went somewhat awry. The professor told me he didn't want to hear a defence of someone who could say that comets are an excrescence in the heavens.[68] He said that you couldn't take someone like that seriously. But of course you have to put this in context, this statement that comets are an excrescence, a sort of rash like measles in the sky. It is so easy to ridicule something, and it may even be delightful to do so. To gain insight into the true workings of the world you don't always have to pull a long face and look deadly earnest. A certain humour is required too, precisely also to understand the full scope of tragedy in the world.

Now after Hegel has given a kind of index of all concepts, all ideas embodied in nature, he rises to the spirit in a third step in his thinking. In the spirit he sees the idea in its intrinsic thusness; that is, it is not as it was before the creation of the world, not only the idea in itself, but now it is the idea existing both *in and for* itself. It lives now in the human soul, and does so for itself: so we have the idea outwardly in objective phenomena, and then also for itself, within the human being. But since the human being is idea—because everything is idea—this is the idea in and for itself. Hegel here tries to trace the idea as it only comes to exist in the soul of the individual human being, and then—though I'm missing out various things—in the state. In the human soul the idea works within; in the state, it has objectivized itself again, living in laws and institutions. The idea inhabits these everywhere, and has assumed objective existence in them. And then it continues to evolve objectively in world history. State, world history. And so now Hegel lists all the ideas in world history that cause humanity's ongoing evolution on the physical plane. All the ideas that live in the soul, the state, in world history, do not however lead us beyond the physical plane, never point us to the possibility of a world of spirit; and this is because, for Hegel, the supersensible world is simply the sum of ideas that live in everything, firstly in their inherent nature before the world was created, then in their externalization in nature, and then in the self-predicated thusness of the human soul in state and world history.

And then the idea evolves to its highest level, in a sense coming to self-awareness, at the ultimate moment of its development, in art, religion and philosophy.

When these three—art, religion and philosophy—manifest in human life, they are superior to state and world history, and yet they are still only the embodiment of pure logic, the embodiment of abstract ideas. In art these ideas, that existed as pure logic before the world was created, represent themselves in the sensory image; in religion through the feeling-imbued idea; and in philosophy the idea, finally, manifests in its pure form in the human mind.

I. Logic: the idea in itself
II. Nature: the idea externalized
III. Spirit: the idea in and for itself   art
      soul—state—world history: religion
                                        philosophy

The human being is fulfilled in philosophy, gazing back upon all else that humanity and nature has produced in the way of ideas, and now feels himself—how shall we put this—as filled by God, who is however also idea, here looking back on its whole preceding development. God regards himself in the human being. But really the idea is regarding itself in the human being. Abstraction regards abstraction.

It is hard to imagine anything more brilliantly abstract. And you can't really conceive of anything more inwardly audacious than to assert that ideas are the most sublime thing, and that apart from these there is no God: the ideas are God, and you, the human soul, are also idea, except that here the idea within you has succeeded in attaining its intrinsic existence in and for itself—it regards itself. You see, we swim in ideas, we ourselves are ideas, everything is idea. This is the world in its most abstract possible form. And it is of huge significance that precisely at the end of the eighteenth century and the beginning of the nineteenth, a mind emerged with the audacity to say that we only grasp reality if we do so in the abstract idea. There is no other higher reality than the abstract idea.

But however hard you search in Hegel's philosophy, what is missing everywhere is any path into the supersensible world. No such path into the supersensible world can exist, for when a person dies—being idea really, as Hegel's philosophy sees it—he enters into the universal stream of world ideas. And we can only speak of this stream of world ideas in this context. In fact the magnificent thing about Hegelian philosophy is that it contains no concept at all of anything supersensible—except that everything we meet in Hegel is already intrinsically supersensible, albeit in the iciest abstraction: supersensible in the abstract. And this turns out to be entirely unfitted for integrating the sensory realm. Things of the senses are spiritualized as supersensible things, albeit only in abstract forms; but at the same time all supersensible reality is dismissed because the sum of ideas, listed from alpha to omega, relates only to the sense world. And so we can say that the supersensible character of these Hegelian ideas becomes relatively insignificant since this supersensible character relates not to a supersensible realm but only to the sense world.

What I want to emphasize here is how modern thinking has tended to entirely dismiss the supersensible, not by a superficial materialism but by the highest potency of spiritual thinking. Hegel is not therefore a materialist but an objective idealist. But this objective idealism asserts that the objective idea is itself God, is the foundation of the world and everything else.

If you trace this spiritual impulse to its conclusion, you find a certain inner satisfaction that allows you to overlook what is missing in Hegel's philosophy. But later thinkers, those who do not think through these ideas in such primary ways, who ponder on them after the event as it were, can feel their deficiencies all the more fully. I have highlighted all these things in my book *The Riddle of Man*.[69]

Now imagine that instead of someone like Hegel, who thinks with an inwardly supersensible impulse, these ideas are taken up by another kind of mind, who really only has a sense of material reality, as was the case with Karl Marx. Then this idealistic philosophy of Hegel's becomes a means to dismiss everything supersensible, and thus also everything idealistic in nature. This is what Karl Marx made of it. Karl Marx appropriated the form of thinking he found in Hegel, except that he did not reflect upon idea within reality but only reality in the sense in which it continually rolls on as merely external, material reality. He perpetuated the Hegelian impulse but materialized it. And thus the very fibre of modern socialist thinking is rooted in the heights of modern idealistic thinking. That the most material thinker of all crossed paths with the most abstract thinker of all was an inner imperative of the nineteenth century, as well as its tragedy. We can say that spiritual life here transformed into its opposite.

Hegel spins a thread of abstract concepts. Being transforms into non-being, cannot endure non-being and thereby enters upon development. In a concatenation of concepts we pass through thesis, antithesis, synthesis in accord with a certain inner triad, which Hegel handles magnificently in the domain of pure idea. Karl Marx overlays this inner triad—which Hegel sought in the inner motion of ideas about logic, nature and mind—on outward, material reality, saying this for instance: that from the modern private capitalist form of human community, there developed (as Hegel develops non-being from being) capitalist socialization of the private capital economy, in the form of trust funds. As these trust funds comprise increasing amounts of company assets, ownership of private capital transforms into its opposite. Associations arise, the opposite of individual capitalism, thus converted into its antithesis. Now comes the synthesis: the whole thing changes again, like non-being into development. The amalgamation of private enterprise into trust fund enterprises transforms into something greater still, which cancels out these trust economies: into public enterprise with the means of production. Thus purely external economic realities are elaborated by Marx, drawn entirely from the Hegelian model, except that Hegel was living in the element of ideas, and Marx in processes of external economics. And so we find two extremes side by side, almost, you might say, like being and non-being.

Dear friends, you can argue for as long as you like about idealism, realism, spirituality and materialism, but you will get nowhere, nowhere at all. The only sustaining thing is to think in terms of the modern trinity: the human being in the middle, with the luciferic on one side, as one extreme, and the ahrimanic as the other extreme on the other. Ahrimanic materialism, luciferic spirituality: the two extremes with the human being as balance in the middle. If you wish to find the truth, you cannot be an idealist, realist, materialist or spiritualist, but must rather be both the one and the other. You must seek the spirit with such intensity that you find this spirit within matter; and you must look through matter keenly enough to find the spirit shining through it. That is our task today: to cease quarrelling about spirituality or materialism but to find the balance. The two extremes, those of Hegelian luciferism and Marxist ahrimanism, have outlived their day. They came to manifest expression. And now the equilibrium, the balance really has to be found—in the form precisely of anthroposophic spiritual science. But to do so we have to ascend to a pure thinking, like that to which Hegel ascended; yet we must be able to use this pure thinking in order to break through to the supersensible. Besides logic—that is, an organism of ideas which can in turn after all only relate to the sense world—we must break through at the place where logic was discovered, the threshold between the sense and the supersensible world. Hegel did not yet manage this breakthrough, and so humanity was repulsed.

You see, in a sense the fact that socialism appeared without any reference to a world of spirit is connected with the purest and noblest aspect of modern thinking. And that it became so difficult in our era for people to complement socialist thinking with spiritual thinking is to some degree part and parcel of humanity's inner path of evolution. But we have to understand the whole context to gain from it the strength to find the next, redemptive step. Academic and scientific study, as practised in the universities of today, has come nowhere near doing so.

What was Hegel's achievement, really? He squeezed the juice from humankind as one squeezes a lemon until it is quite dry—not physically of course but ideally. And this eviscerated lemon of humanity becomes in the end nothing but an idea. Here you sit before me on chairs; in terms of Hegel's philosophy you are all ideas sitting here, not bodies at all, not souls: ideas. Each of you bears within you an idea that existed as abstract idea before the world was created. Then each one of you is a separate body, embodied in nature: the idea in its externalization and extrapolation sits here on these chairs. But then in turn the idea is in you in its intrinsic thusness, or being in and for itself. You yourself comprehend this idea, which is you. Just consider what a spectre you are! Picture how squeezed out you are when you sit here as 'idea': you are inherently idea, externalized idea, an idea in and for itself—and yet nothing but idea!

And when we come to Karl Marx, the ideas have all gone—precisely because he passed through the method of Hegelian idealism. You have now become nothing but a two-legged animal, only what manifests outwardly in the natural order: the other extreme!

Surely, given what has come about in humanity's evolution, an attempt should now be made to regain a view and vision of the *human* within the human being; or in other words, to establish the essence of the human being not merely as a universal idea, nor as a merely animal creature, but the real, individual, embodied human being, who is the apex of nature, who bears within him a soul being which has become the aim and destination of a world of spirit. Human vision should be directed once again to the real and actual human being—something I attempted in my *Philosophy of Freedom*.[70] This is the real historical context of the problem that posed itself when I felt compelled to write *The Philosophy of Freedom*. This very highly developed animal creature in which the human being is embodied cannot be free; nor can that spectral human be free who is absolute idea—idea in itself, idea externalized, and idea in and for itself—since this idea has been formed by logical imperative. Neither of these is free. Only the real human being is free, seen as the poise and equilibrium between the idea—which does however break through to real spirit—and outward material realities.

That is why I tried in *The Philosophy of Freedom* to found ethical life not on some kind of abstract principle but on our inner moral experience, which I called 'moral imagination'; on that aspect in our intrinsically human, individual being which draws on Intuition. Kant established the categorical imperative to act so that the principles of your actions can be a guideline for all other people.[71] 'Put on a coat that can fit all others!' But the maxim of the philosophy of freedom says, 'Act as the spirit directs you, in your highest human powers, in the specific moment, in the individual, tangible moment.'

In this way, via moral philosophy, we arrive at spirituality. And a path to comprehend the spiritual world would open up for modern humanity if people could see—and this is not really so difficult to grasp—that the ethical dimension has no secure foundation unless regarded as part of a supersensible, spiritual realm.

Hegel's logic is from beginning to end a sum of abstract ideas. Ultimately there is little harm done by regarding all of nature, all palpable and superficial existence, only as a schema of ideas. But harm is done if the impulses for our ethical actions do not come from the spiritual world, since these impulses then have no true reality at all, are only so much vapour and noise issuing from the human animal creature. When the animal human dies, nothing remains. In Hegel's philosophy there is nothing anywhere relating to any aspect of human existence after we pass through the gate of death, or before we pass through the gate of birth. Hegelian philosophy is grandiose, but only as a point of transition in the nineteenth century. Acknowledging Hegel's greatness leads us to the need to take him further, to break through the barrier that we find when we engage with pure thinking, pure logic, with the idea in itself—and enter the supersensible world. To be a Hegelian today can only be a sort of private indulgence for a few ratiocinating minds who, at the outset of this twentieth century, seek their mental ingenuity in adopting a position that was only fitting for the first few decades of the nineteenth. My dear friends, we must learn not to live only in the abstract but to live in time, in temporal developments. By so doing we engage with living realities, rejecting absolutisms which will not enable us to collaborate in actual human progress—which is precisely what we need to do.

Look, Raphael was a great man. The Sistine Madonna is a major work of creative genius. But you can only properly appraise it if you recognize that someone who painted it today would have created a poor work. We must not be absolutist but know how to place ourselves into the great context of humanity's evolution. To disregard this is to transgress seriously, is the real harm done in our era. Today it is imperative to relinquish absolute positions, which were permissible in earlier periods. In the age of the consciousness soul it is vital to be aware of the nature of the times in which a particular incarnation has placed us. However paradoxical this sounds, we can only rightly appraise Raphael's Sistine Madonna if we were also willing to regard the same painting as poor if a modern painter created it today, because the times have moved on. Nothing has absolute validity. Things have value for their place and time. Previously this was not an essential insight, but it has now become so, and after all it is not unfathomably profound. It was a great achievement of Pythagoras to come up with his theorem when he did. If someone were to invent or discover it today, it would merely be interesting, don't you think? It would also be merely interesting if someone were to paint the Sistine Madonna today; and this is because it is no longer the time for this; it is not what has to happen at the point of evolution where we now are.

You can see, my dear friends, how thinking must be reformed, how thought must be socialized. We need to gain a felt sense of developing humanity, though this is something that will appear paradoxical to most people today. But that is really what is needed: to radically change our thinking, to arrive at really new thoughts. The old ideas will not sustain us any more. If people go on spinning their old thoughts, the world will inevitably collapse around them. The salvation of humanity depends on people being able to relinquish their old ways of thinking and seek a thinking that is truly new. Spiritual science is a new way of thinking, and it is disparaged so much precisely because it runs counter, really, to all the old habits of thought. Only those who have a sense of the need to develop new thinking will come to a proper appraisal of spiritual science in general and also of its revelations in specific realms of life, for instance the social question.

But there is another thing too that constitutes the unhealthy nature of our modern era: that subconsciously people are already embarking on a different way of thinking but, through a kind of historical obstinacy, suppress this and in consequence suffer the inevitable penalties of suppressed thinking. Developments and occurrences in modern history are largely a penalty for wayward human nature, which suppresses what lies in the depths below and cling by a kind of simulation to what they have clung to for centuries. It is worth studying, particularly, the rigorous and consistent thinkers of the previous era—not the inconsistent and lazy ones—and you will find in their works how wrong paths were taken. The previous era was characterized by thinkers who stood firm on the foundations of the past rather than by those who made tiny concessions to modernism. Many years ago a gathering was convened in Austria, where all the abstract minds who vaunted progress and liberal values were discussing how religion must be transformed to meet the needs of a new era—in other words the same tune sung continually by all petty bourgeois minds from Gladstone[72] through to the respectable parliamentarians of Europe. At this, Cardinal Rauscher[73] stood up and waved the great flag of old-fashioned ecclesiasticism. The Catholic Church, he said, did not acknowledge progress; what had once been true will remain so for all ages. Nothing new that contradicts it has any validity. Thus spoke the consummate spirit of the old era. Similarly there was Pobedonostsev,[74] the only figure to condemn the whole of modern western culture in a brilliant and inventive manner. In his view, this culture would and could lead nowhere. The old order, to which the modern bourgeoisie has become so accustomed, could only be sustained if they wished to shape the world as Cardinal Rauscher and Pobedonostsev himself wished to shape it. If the rigid principles of Pobedonostsev had really been imposed on the world, instead of the wishy-washy ones of Tsar Nicholas II,[75] the war would of course never have happened. Except that nothing could actually have been achieved by Pobedonostsev's ideas since the world and reality itself took a different course. And the important thing is to follow the path of reality—not by making little concessions and appeasements, not by behaving as most figures did in the second half of the nineteenth century or even in the first two decades of the twentieth, but by really resolving upon a way of thinking that is as different from earlier forms as, putting it negatively, the devastation of the world war differs from the conditions that prevailed beforehand. We ought at least to learn one thing from the terrible disaster humanity has suffered, which people keep saying is the worst calamity there has ever been in history: we should learn that it is high time to formulate thoughts that have likewise never previously existed.

It is time for humanity to make a great resolve. Basically the socialism rearing its head is something that arises unconsciously from human instincts and seeks to bring this resolve to fruition. But the world will not emerge from chaos until a sufficient number of people add an ideal spirituality to material socialism. Thus are things connected in our time. But until people can see the reality in front of their noses, human society will find no redemption as it develops. Perceiving reality should become, in a sense, our inner soul practice, drawn from the impulses of spiritual science. I want to keep trying to urge you to embrace this inner soul practice. The more you come to feel that such a thing is essential today, as I have again tried to impress on you in our reflections today, the more fully and rightly you will join with the spiritual stream that looks to anthroposophically oriented spiritual science for its source of vitality.

Next Friday I will speak further of this.[76]

NOTES

Original text: this was taken down in shorthand and typed up—like almost all lectures from 1916 onwards which Steiner gave in Dornach and many other places—by the stenographer Helen Finckh (1883–1960). The first edition of the lectures in the Collected Works (GA) drew on these original transcripts. The editions published in 1946 and 1957 were prepared by Marie Steiner and C. von Steiger.

Works by Rudolf Steiner referred to in the text, which are part of the GA (Collected Works) are cited with GA number.

1. The lectures given in Dornach include: GA 185a and GA 186. The public lectures in Zurich were published in GA 328; lectures in Bern (6 and 7 February), Basel (13 and 14 February), and Wintherthur (26 February and 19 March) have not yet been published.
2. Councillor of Commerce Dr. Emil Molt, 1876–1936, owned the Waldorf-Astoria cigarette factory, collaborated actively in the threefold movement, and founded the first Waldorf school in Stuttgart (1919). It was at his request that Rudolf Steiner oversaw the founding and running of the school.
   Dr. Roman Boos, 1889–1952, was a social scientist, writer and speaker who strongly promoted anthroposophy and the threefolding idea. Between 1930 and 1934 he directed the Social Sciences Association at the Goetheanum in Dornach.
   Hans Kühn, 1889–1977, was a writer and publisher (Columban-Verlag Arlesheim). See his book, *Dreigliederungszeit. Rudolf Steiners Kampf für die Gesellschaftsordnung der Zukunft*, Dornach 1978.
3. After the Compiégne armistice between the central and western powers, no real peace conference took place. The Paris peace conference that began in Versailles on 18 January 1919 was only a gathering of delegates from the 27 entente states for the purpose of deciding upon conditions to be imposed on the central axis powers.
4. International Socialists Conference in Bern, from 3 to 10 February 1919.
5. On 13 February, in 'The Real Shape of Social Questions, Arising from the Existential Needs of Modern Humanity' (unpublished).
6. Lectures published in GA 187 (8 lectures in Basel and Dornach, 1918/1919).
7. Article by the economist and statesman Walter Rathenau, 1867–1922, from the *Neue Zürcher Zeitung*, no. 1734, 28 December 1918.
8. 'An Appeal to the Civilized World', 4 October 1914, signed by almost all leading minds in Germany and translated into ten languages. See *Der Krieg der Geister. Deutsche und ausländische Stimmen zum Weltkriege*, ed. by Dr. Hermann Kellermann, Weimar/Dresden 1915.

9. The appeal 'To the German People and the Civilized World' was published as a leaflet in Stuttgart and disseminated from 5 March onwards, also appearing in many daily newspapers in Germany, Austria and Switzerland. Rudolf Steiner included it in his book *Towards Social Renewal* (GA 23).
10. Dr Walter Johannes Stein, 1891–1957, a teacher at the Stuttgart Waldorf School, writer and speaker.
11. In his lectures of 1918, Steiner keeps mentioning this fact. See in particular the lecture of 24 November 1918. Concerning the emergence of the idea of threefolding in 1917, and efforts to gain public interest in this, see: R. Steiner 'Memoranda of July 1917' in GA 24; Roman Boos (ed.), *Rudolf Steiner während des Weltkrieges*, Dornach 1933; Hella Wiesberger, 'Das Jahr 1917. Im Gedenken an ein geistes- und weltgeschichtliches Ereignis', newsletter of the Rudolf Steiner Estate, issue 15, summer 1966, p. 1–14; and Hella Wiesberger, 'Rudolf Steiners öffentliches Wirken für die Dreigliederung des sozialen Organimus. Von der Dreigliederungs-Idee des Jahres 1917 zur Dreigliederungs-Bewegung des Jahres 1919.', ibid, issue 24/25, Easter 1969, p. 6–31.
12. Woodrow Wilson, 1856–1924, President of the USA from 1913 to 1921.
13. On 20 or 21 January a conversation took place on social threefolding between Steiner and Prince Max von Baden, who was later to be German Chancellor. For more on this see H. Kühn, *Dreigliederungszeit* (see note 2), p. 18; and H. Wiesberger, 'Eine Chronik' (see note 11).
14. The person in question remains unknown.
15. Erich Ludendorff, 1865–1937, in 1916 Quartermaster General, and chief aid to Hindenburg in the First World War.
16. The lecture was prefaced by a few words from Roman Boos and Rudolf Steiner concerning the 'Appeal' (see page 7ff). Rudolf Steiner's words were as follows: 'It may be unnecessary to say that the whole matter must remain completely confidential for the time being. Please do not show the appeal to outsiders therefore. In general, also, there will be no need to give a copy of this appeal to everyone, but there will be an opportunity for you to read it at Herr L's house. In a few days, in a short time, it will be published in the newspapers. Outsiders should not be informed of it [in advance] for otherwise certain circles will get wind of it, which may lead to prejudice and preconceptions developing. When the appeal is published people can acquaint themselves with it as it stands and see the names of signatories. The important thing is not that the appeal should be proclaimed to persuade people or in some way change their minds, but that it is accompanied by a certain number of signatures so that people can see straight away that there really is some impetus behind this, represented by a number of people. And that is why the appeal without the signatures should not be made public in advance in some way.'
17. See here lecture 14 in Rudolf Steiner, *World Economy*, vol. I, GA 340.
18. See the lecture of 29 December 1918 in GA 187.
19. Adolf Harnack, 1851–1930, *Das Wesen des Christentums*, 4th edition Leipzig 1901.
20. Matthew 28:20.
21. Matthew 25:40.

22. Woodrow Wilson, *The New Freedom, A Call for the Emancipation of the Generous Energies of a People*, New York 1913.
23. See, for instance, the lecture of 12 January 1923 in GA 220.
24. Lecture of 14 February, on 'Attempts at Solutions for Social Questions' (unpublished).
25. See Rudolf Steiner's article 'A Society for Ethical Culture' in GA 31.
26. See the chapter 'World Evolution and the Human Being' in *Occult Science, An Outline*, GA 13.
27. Karl Marx, 1818–83.
28. Vladimir I. Lenin, 1870–1924.
29. David Ricardo, 1772–1823, an English economist. His major work is *Principles of Political Economy and Taxation*, 1817.
30. Friedrich Engels, 1820–95.
31. See the lecture by Emil Du Bois-Reymond, 'On the Limits of Natural Science', given on 14 August 1872. The lecture was published in German in Leipzig in 1872. On page 45, it says: 'As regards the enigma of the corporeal world, the natural investigator has long been accustomed to utter his "Ignoramus" with masculine renunciation. Looking back on the continuous course of success, he is sustained in this acknowledgement by the quiet awareness that, although he does not presently know, he might at least know under different circumstances, and may perhaps at last come to know. But concerning the enigma of the nature of matter and energy, and how we are to conceive of them, he must resolve once and for all to utter the much harder truth of "Ignorabimus"!'
32. Ferdinand Lasalle, 1825–64, co-founder of German Social Democracy.
33. V.I. Lenin, *The State and Revolution, the Marxist Theory of the State and The Tasks of the Proletariat in the Revolution*, 1917.
34. The central character in Shakespeare's *The Merchant of Venice*.
35. Cameralistics: the science of public finance. From the 18th century onwards, this was a subject taught at universities, and included theories of trade, finance and administration as a preparation for a career in state administration.
36. Lecture given on 22 September 1901: 'How is scientific socialism possible?' There is no extant transcript.
37. Dr. Carl Unger, 1878–1929, engineer. An active proponent of anthroposophy in Germany. From 1912 to 1923 a member of the Executive Council (Vorstand) of the Anthroposophical Society. In 1914/1915 he supervised the building of the first Goetheanum.
38. *Towards Social Renewal*, GA 23. The Zurich lectures originally appeared under the title 'The Social Question', in GA 238.
39. After the lecture, Steiner announced that he would have to travel to Zurich for a eurythmy performance there on 24 February and a lecture to students on 25 February. On 26 February he would give a lecture in Winterthur, and would only be back in Dornach on 28 February, in time for a public lecture in Basel.
40. The evening had begun with a recitation of poems by Conrad Ferdinand Meyer given by Marie Steiner-von Sivers. These were poems 'which all relate to certain deeper experiences connected with death' (Rudolf Steiner's intro-

ductory phrase). The poems were: 'Over a Grave', 'Lethe', 'To a Dead Woman', 'The End of the Festival' and 'Dying Medusa'.
41. In Marxism, the theory of added value refers to the difference between the value of output and the wage the worker receives. Marxism teaches that the worker is wrongly deprived of this added value by the capitalist system. The idea is elaborated in Karl Marx's major work *Capital, A Critique of Political Economy*, London 1867.
42. GA 18.
43. See note 26.
44. Christian Freiherr von Wolf, 1679–1754, *Vernünftige Gedanken von Gott, der Welt und der Seele des Menschen, auch allen Dingen überhaupt*, 1719. By 1732 this book had already reached its fifth edition.
45. The first Goetheanum, a double cupola structure built in wood to house the School of Spiritual Science in Dornach. It was burned down in an arson attack at New Year 1922/23. See GA 286 and 290 (lecture on 29 June 1921 in Bern).
46. 'Dieterich pours contempt over all men who simply investigate comets as natural objects, calling special attention to a comet then in the heavens resembling a long broom or bundle of rods and declares that he and his hearers can only consider it rightly "when we see standing before us our Lord God in heaven as an angry father with a rod for his children."'
See http://www.godrules.net/library/white/100white24.htm
47. Leo Davidovitch Trotsky, 1879–1940.
48. Johann Gottlieb Fichte, 1762–1814, *Der geschlossene Handelstaat, ein philosophischer Entwurf einer künftig zu liefernden Politik*, 1800.
49. See especially the lecture in Berlin on 16 December 1915 in GA 65. Also *The Riddles of Philosophy* (1914), GA 18 (index) and GA 20, Chapter Two.
50. See for instance GA 177 and 178. Also GA 185.
51. On 28 February: 'The Social Question as Question of Economics, Rights and Culture' (unpublished).
52. See GA 328, especially the lectures of 10, 12 and 25 February.
53. Kurt Eisner, 1867–1919, socialist leader, journalist, writer. As Prime Minster of the Bavarian government he was murdered on 21 February 1921. Shortly before this, on 10 February, he gave a lecture at the invitation of a Basel student group on 'Socialism and Youth', and Rudolf Steiner quotes from this (Basel 1919, p. 13). It is worth noting that Steiner had a conversation with Kurt Eisner, about the question of war guilt, on 6 or 7 February during the Bern socialist congress. See Hans Kühn, *Dreigliederungszeit*, p. 33ff.
54. See the lecture of 14 April 1914 in GA 153, where Steiner says (p. 174/175 of the German edition): 'Today therefore, production for the market proceeds without regard to consumption, at odds with what I elaborated in my essay on "Spiritual Science and the Social Question". Everything that is produced is instead stacked up in warehouses and via currency markets, and then people wait to see how much is bought. This tendency will keep increasing until—and when I say this, you will soon discover why—it destroys itself. This type of production arising in society, in the social fabric of human beings on earth, is exactly the same thing as a carcinoma that develops in an organism. Exactly

the same: a cancer, a carcinoma, cultural cancer, cultural carcinoma! With spiritual insight into society one can perceive this cancer, can see the terrible predisposition being created for social tumours to thrive. Someone who can see what is happening will feel this deep concern for our culture. It is a terrible thing, and feels very oppressive; and even if one might perhaps otherwise suppress all one's enthusiasm for spiritual science, and silence every impulse to speak up for it, an outcry must be made against this ever-strengthening tendency. We cannot be silent. This demands a potent remedy. Something that must occupy its own distinct sphere—like that in which nature is creatively active—in the dissemination of spiritual truths, becomes a carcinoma when it infiltrates culture in the way I have described.' In the collected essays from the journal *Luzifer-Gnosis*, GA 34.

55. Fritz Mauthner, 1849–1923, *Wörterbuch der Philosophie. Neue Beiträge zu einer Kritik der Sprache*, 2 vols., Leipzig and Munich 1910 and 1911.
56. GA 9.
57. This might be the pacifist Professor Friedrich Wilhelm Foerster, a German delegate at the international socialist conference in Bern (3 to 10 February). See his essays on 'Christ and the War' and 'Christ the Organizer' in Friedrich W. Foerster, *Die deutsche Jugend und der Weltkrieg*, Leipzig 1916. Concerning Steiner's attempt to have a discussion with him, see H. Kühn, *Dreigliederungszeit*, p. 36.
58. We were unable to locate the source of this quote.
59. At the socialist conference; see note 57.
60. Gottlieb von Jagow, 1863–1935, was German Foreign Secretary from 1913 to 1916.
61. This took place from 7 to 13 March. See Rudolf Steiner's lecture of 11 March 1919 in Bern, 'The True Foundation for a League of Nations in the Economic, Juristic and Spiritual Powers of the Nations', published in *Gegenwart* 1943/44, no. 8/9, and as a single-lecture edition in Bern in 1944.
62. Johannes Ude, born 1874, Catholic theologian and spokesman on sociopolitics.
63. This has increased today to between 50 and 75 years after the author's death.
64. See note 61.
65. Rudolf Steiner often spoke of this metamorphosis, for instance in GA 170, 191, and elsewhere.
66. *The Speeches of Woodrow Wilson*, published by the Committee on Public Information of the United States of America (English and German), Bern 1919 (Der freie Verlag); speech of 22 January 1917.
67. Walther Schücking, 1875–1935, expert on international law.
68. Steiner could be thinking of the following passage in Hegel's *Lectures on Natural Philosophy* (§ 268): 'The fulfilment of space erupts in an infinite variety of materials; but this is only the first eruption that can delight our gaze (the hosts of stars). This eruption of light is as little worthy of wonder as the rash on human skin, or as a quantity of flies.' (*Hegels Werke*, complete [German] edition, vol. 7, Berlin 1847, ed. By C.L. Michelet.
69. GA 20.
70. GA 4.

71. In various formulations, for instance in *Critique of Practical Reason* (1788), Part I, § 7: 'Act in such a way that the maxims of your will could at any moment hold good as the principle of a general law.'
72. William Gladstone, 1809–98, British Prime Minister.
73. Cardinal Joseph Othmar von Rauscher, 1797–1875, Archbishop of Vienna.
74. Konstantin Petrovich Pobedonostsev, 1827–1907, Russian jurist and influential statesman.
75. Tsar Nicholas II, 1868–1918, ruled from 1894 to 1917; from 1905 under the influence of Pobedonostsev.
76. The continuing lectures of the series, from 21 March, are contained in GA 190.

RUDOLF STEINER'S COLLECTED WORKS

The German Edition of Rudolf Steiner's Collected Works (the *Gesamtausgabe* [GA] published by Rudolf Steiner Verlag, Dornach, Switzerland) presently runs to 354 titles, organized either by type of work (written or spoken), chronology, audience (public or other), or subject (education, art, etc.). For ease of comparison, the Collected Works in English [CW] follows the German organization exactly. A complete listing of the CWs follows with literal translations of the German titles. Other than in the case of the books published in his lifetime, titles were rarely given by Rudolf Steiner himself, and were often provided by the editors of the German editions. The titles in English are not necessarily the same as the German; and, indeed, over the past seventy-five years have frequently been different, with the same book sometimes appearing under different titles.

For ease of identification and to avoid confusion, we suggest that readers looking for a title should do so by CW number. Because the work of creating the Collected Works of Rudolf Steiner is an ongoing process, with new titles being published every year, we have not indicated in this listing which books are presently available. To find out what titles in the Collected Works are currently in print, please check our website at www.rudolfsteinerpress.com (or www.steinerbooks.org for US readers).

Written Work

CW 1	Goethe: Natural-Scientific Writings, Introduction, with Footnotes and Explanations in the text by Rudolf Steiner
CW 2	Outlines of an Epistemology of the Goethean World View, with Special Consideration of Schiller
CW 3	Truth and Science
CW 4	The Philosophy of Freedom
CW 4a	Documents to 'The Philosophy of Freedom'
CW 5	Friedrich Nietzsche, A Fighter against His Time
CW 6	Goethe's Worldview
CW 6a	Now in CW 30
CW 7	Mysticism at the Dawn of Modern Spiritual Life and Its Relationship with Modern Worldviews
CW 8	Christianity as Mystical Fact and the Mysteries of Antiquity
CW 9	Theosophy: An Introduction into Supersensible World Knowledge and Human Purpose
CW 10	How Does One Attain Knowledge of Higher Worlds?
CW 11	From the Akasha-Chronicle

CW 12	Levels of Higher Knowledge
CW 13	Occult Science in Outline
CW 14	Four Mystery Dramas
CW 15	The Spiritual Guidance of the Individual and Humanity
CW 16	A Way to Human Self-Knowledge: Eight Meditations
CW 17	The Threshold of the Spiritual World. Aphoristic Comments
CW 18	The Riddles of Philosophy in Their History, Presented as an Outline
CW 19	Contained in CW 24
CW 20	The Riddles of the Human Being: Articulated and Unarticulated in the Thinking, Views and Opinions of a Series of German and Austrian Personalities
CW 21	The Riddles of the Soul
CW 22	Goethe's Spiritual Nature And Its Revelation In 'Faust' and through the 'Fairy Tale of the Snake and the Lily'
CW 23	The Central Points of the Social Question in the Necessities of Life in the Present and the Future
CW 24	Essays Concerning the Threefold Division of the Social Organism and the Period 1915–1921
CW 25	Cosmology, Religion and Philosophy
CW 26	Anthroposophical Leading Thoughts
CW 27	Fundamentals for Expansion of the Art of Healing according to Spiritual-Scientific Insights
CW 28	The Course of My Life
CW 29	Collected Essays on Dramaturgy, 1889–1900
CW 30	Methodical Foundations of Anthroposophy: Collected Essays on Philosophy, Natural Science, Aesthetics and Psychology, 1884–1901
CW 31	Collected Essays on Culture and Current Events, 1887–1901
CW 32	Collected Essays on Literature, 1884–1902
CW 33	Biographies and Biographical Sketches, 1894–1905
CW 34	Lucifer-Gnosis: Foundational Essays on Anthroposophy and Reports from the Periodicals 'Lucifer' and 'Lucifer-Gnosis,' 1903–1908
CW 35	Philosophy and Anthroposophy: Collected Essays, 1904–1923
CW 36	The Goetheanum-Idea in the Middle of the Cultural Crisis of the Present: Collected Essays from the Periodical 'Das Goetheanum,' 1921–1925
CW 37	Now in CWs 260a and 251
CW 38	Letters, Vol. 1: 1881–1890
CW 39	Letters, Vol. 2: 1890–1925
CW 40	Truth-Wrought Words
CW 40a	Sayings, Poems and Mantras; Supplementary Volume
CW 42	Now in CWs 264–266
CW 43	Stage Adaptations
CW 44	On the Four Mystery Dramas. Sketches, Fragments and Paralipomena on the Four Mystery Dramas
CW 45	Anthroposophy: A Fragment from the Year 1910

Rudolf Steiner's Collected Works * 143

Public Lectures

CW 51	On Philosophy, History and Literature
CW 52	Spiritual Teachings Concerning the Soul and Observation of the World
CW 53	The Origin and Goal of the Human Being
CW 54	The Riddles of the World and Anthroposophy
CW 55	Knowledge of the Supersensible in Our Times and Its Meaning for Life Today
CW 56	Knowledge of the Soul and of the Spirit
CW 57	Where and How Does One Find the Spirit?
CW 58	The Metamorphoses of the Soul Life. Paths of Soul Experiences: Part One
CW 59	The Metamorphoses of the Soul Life. Paths of Soul Experiences: Part Two
CW 60	The Answers of Spiritual Science to the Biggest Questions of Existence
CW 61	Human History in the Light of Spiritual Research
CW 62	Results of Spiritual Research
CW 63	Spiritual Science as a Treasure for Life
CW 64	Out of Destiny-Burdened Times
CW 65	Out of Central European Spiritual Life
CW 66	Spirit and Matter, Life and Death
CW 67	The Eternal in the Human Soul. Immortality and Freedom
CW 68	Public lectures in various cities, 1906–1918
CW 69	Public lectures in various cities, 1906–1918
CW 70	Public lectures in various cities, 1906–1918
CW 71	Public lectures in various cities, 1906–1918
CW 72	Freedom—Immortality—Social Life
CW 73	The Supplementing of the Modern Sciences through Anthroposophy
CW 73a	Specialized Fields of Knowledge and Anthroposophy
CW 74	The Philosophy of Thomas Aquinas
CW 75	Public lectures in various cities, 1906–1918
CW 76	The Fructifying Effect of Anthroposophy on Specialized Fields
CW 77a	The Task of Anthroposophy in Relation to Science and Life: The Darmstadt College Course
CW 77b	Art and Anthroposophy. The Goetheanum-Impulse
CW 78	Anthroposophy, Its Roots of Knowledge and Fruits for Life
CW 79	The Reality of the Higher Worlds
CW 80	Public lectures in various cities, 1922
CW 81	Renewal-Impulses for Culture and Science—Berlin College Course
CW 82	So that the Human Being Can Become a Complete Human Being
CW 83	Western and Eastern World-Contrast. Paths to Understanding It through Anthroposophy
CW 84	What Did the Goetheanum Intend and What Should Anthroposophy Do?

Lectures to the Members of the Anthroposophical Society

CW 88	Concerning the Astral World and Devachan
CW 89	Consciousness—Life—Form. Fundamental Principles of a Spiritual-Scientific Cosmology
CW 90	Participant Notes from the Lectures during the Years 1903–1905
CW 91	Participant Notes from the Lectures during the Years 1903–1905
CW 92	The Occult Truths of Ancient Myths and Sagas
CW 93	The Temple Legend and the Golden Legend
CW 93a	Fundamentals of Esotericism
CW 94	Cosmogony. Popular Occultism. The Gospel of John. The Theosophy in the Gospel of John
CW 95	At the Gates of Theosophy
CW 96	Origin-Impulses of Spiritual Science. Christian Esotericism in the Light of New Spirit-Knowledge
CW 97	The Christian Mystery
CW 98	Nature Beings and Spirit Beings—Their Effects in Our Visible World
CW 99	The Theosophy of the Rosicrucians
CW 100	Human Development and Christ-Knowledge
CW 101	Myths and Legends. Occult Signs and Symbols
CW 102	The Working into Human Beings by Spiritual Beings
CW 103	The Gospel of John
CW 104	The Apocalypse of John
CW 104a	From the Picture-Script of the Apocalypse of John
CW 105	Universe, Earth, the Human Being: Their Being and Development, as well as Their Reflection in the Connection between Egyptian Mythology and Modern Culture
CW 106	Egyptian Myths and Mysteries in Relation to the Active Spiritual Forces of the Present
CW 107	Spiritual-Scientific Knowledge of the Human Being
CW 108	Answering the Questions of Life and the World through Anthroposophy
CW 109	The Principle of Spiritual Economy in Connection with the Question of Reincarnation. An Aspect of the Spiritual Guidance of Humanity
CW 110	The Spiritual Hierarchies and Their Reflection in the Physical World. Zodiac, Planets and Cosmos
CW 111	Contained in CW 109
CW 112	The Gospel of John in Relation to the Three Other Gospels, Especially the Gospel of Luke
CW 113	The Orient in the Light of the Occident. The Children of Lucifer and the Brothers of Christ
CW 114	The Gospel of Luke
CW 115	Anthroposophy—Psychosophy—Pneumatosophy
CW 116	The Christ-Impulse and the Development of 'I'-Consciousness
CW 117	The Deeper Secrets of the Development of Humanity in Light of the Gospels

CW 118	The Event of the Christ-Appearance in the Etheric World
CW 119	Macrocosm and Microcosm. The Large World and the Small World. Soul-Questions, Life-Questions, Spirit-Questions
CW 120	The Revelation of Karma
CW 121	The Mission of Individual Folk-Souls in Connection with Germanic-Nordic Mythology
CW 122	The Secrets of the Biblical Creation-Story. The Six-Day Work in the First Book of Moses
CW 123	The Gospel of Matthew
CW 124	Excursus in the Area of the Gospel of Mark
CW 125	Paths and Goals of the Spiritual Human Being. Life Questions in the Light of Spiritual Science
CW 126	Occult History. Esoteric Observations of the Karmic Relationships of Personalities and Events of World History
CW 127	The Mission of the New Spiritual Revelation. The Christ-Event as the Middle-Point of Earth Evolution
CW 128	An Occult Physiology
CW 129	Wonders of the World, Trials of the Soul, and Revelations of the Spirit
CW 130	Esoteric Christianity and the Spiritual Guidance of Humanity
CW 131	From Jesus to Christ
CW 132	Evolution from the View Point of the Truth
CW 133	The Earthly and the Cosmic Human Being
CW 134	The World of the Senses and the World of the Spirit
CW 135	Reincarnation and Karma and their Meaning for the Culture of the Present
CW 136	The Spiritual Beings in Celestial Bodies and the Realms of Nature
CW 137	The Human Being in the Light of Occultism, Theosophy and Philosophy
CW 138	On Initiation. On Eternity and the Passing Moment. On the Light of the Spirit and the Darkness of Life
CW 139	The Gospel of Mark
CW 140	Occult Investigation into the Life between Death and New Birth. The Living Interaction between Life and Death
CW 141	Life between Death and New Birth in Relationship to Cosmic Facts
CW 142	The Bhagavad Gita and the Letters of Paul
CW 143	Experiences of the Supersensible. Three Paths of the Soul to Christ
CW 144	The Mysteries of the East and of Christianity
CW 145	What Significance Does Occult Development of the Human Being Have for the Sheaths—Physical Body, Etheric Body, Astral Body, and Self?
CW 146	The Occult Foundations of the Bhagavad Gita
CW 147	The Secrets of the Threshold
CW 148	Out of Research in the Akasha: The Fifth Gospel
CW 149	Christ and the Spiritual World. Concerning the Search for the Holy Grail

CW 150	The World of the Spirit and Its Extension into Physical Existence; The Influence of the Dead in the World of the Living
CW 151	Human Thought and Cosmic Thought
CW 152	Preliminary Stages to the Mystery of Golgotha
CW 153	The Inner Being of the Human Being and Life Between Death and New Birth
CW 154	How does One Gain an Understanding of the Spiritual World? The Flowing in of Spiritual Impulses from out of the World of the Deceased
CW 155	Christ and the Human Soul. Concerning the Meaning of Life. Theosophical Morality. Anthroposophy and Christianity
CW 156	Occult Reading and Occult Hearing
CW 157	Human Destinies and the Destiny of Peoples
CW 157a	The Formation of Destiny and the Life after Death
CW 158	The Connection Between the Human Being and the Elemental World. Kalevala—Olaf Åsteson—The Russian People—The World as the Result of the Influences of Equilibrium
CW 159	The Mystery of Death. The Nature and Significance of Middle Europe and the European Folk Spirits
CW 160	In CW 159
CW 161	Paths of Spiritual Knowledge and the Renewal of the Artistic Worldview
CW 162	Questions of Art and Life in Light of Spiritual Science
CW 163	Coincidence, Necessity and Providence. Imaginative Knowledge and the Processes after Death
CW 164	The Value of Thinking for a Knowledge That Satisfies the Human Being. The Relationship of Spiritual Science to Natural Science
CW 165	The Spiritual Unification of Humanity through the Christ-Impulse
CW 166	Necessity and Freedom in the Events of the World and in Human Action
CW 167	The Present and the Past in the Human Spirit
CW 168	The Connection between the Living and the Dead
CW 169	World-being and Selfhood
CW 170	The Riddle of the Human Being. The Spiritual Background of Human History. Cosmic and Human History, Vol. 1
CW 171	Inner Development-Impulses of Humanity. Goethe and the Crisis of the 19th Century. Cosmic and Human History, Vol. 2
CW 172	The Karma of the Vocation of the Human Being in Connection with Goethe's Life. Cosmic and Human History, Vol. 3
CW 173	Contemporary-Historical Considerations: The Karma of Untruthfulness, Part One. Cosmic and Human History, Vol. 4
CW 174	Contemporary-Historical Considerations: The Karma of Untruthfulness, Part Two. Cosmic and Human History, Vol. 5
CW 174a	Middle Europe between East and West. Cosmic and Human History, Vol. 6
CW 174b	The Spiritual Background of the First World War. Cosmic and Human History, Vol. 7

CW 175	Building Stones for an Understanding of the Mystery of Golgotha. Cosmic and Human Metamorphoses
CW 176	Truths of Evolution of the Individual and Humanity. The Karma of Materialism
CW 177	The Spiritual Background of the Outer World. The Fall of the Spirits of Darkness. Spiritual Beings and Their Effects, Vol. 1
CW 178	Individual Spiritual Beings and their Influence in the Soul of the Human Being. Spiritual Beings and their Effects, Vol. 2
CW 179	Spiritual Beings and Their Effects. Historical Necessity and Freedom. The Influences on Destiny from out of the World of the Dead. Spiritual Beings and Their Effects, Vol. 3
CW 180	Mystery Truths and Christmas Impulses. Ancient Myths and their Meaning. Spiritual Beings and Their Effects, Vol. 4
CW 181	Earthly Death and Cosmic Life. Anthroposophical Gifts for Life. Necessities of Consciousness for the Present and the Future.
CW 182	Death as Transformation of Life
CW 183	The Science of the Development of the Human Being
CW 184	The Polarity of Duration and Development in Human Life. The Cosmic Pre-History of Humanity
CW 185	Historical Symptomology
CW 185a	Historical-Developmental Foundations for Forming a Social Judgement
CW 186	The Fundamental Social Demands of Our Time—In Changed Situations
CW 187	How Can Humanity Find the Christ Again? The Threefold Shadow-Existence of our Time and the New Christ-Light
CW 188	Goetheanism, a Transformation-Impulse and Resurrection-Thought. Science of the Human Being and Science of Sociology
CW 189	The Social Question as a Question of Consciousness. The Spiritual Background of the Social Question, Vol. 1
CW 190	Impulses of the Past and the Future in Social Occurrences. The Spiritual Background of the Social Question, Vol. 2
CW 191	Social Understanding from Spiritual-Scientific Cognition. The Spiritual Background of the Social Question, Vol. 3
CW 192	Spiritual-Scientific Treatment of Social and Pedagogical Questions
CW 193	The Inner Aspect of the Social Riddle. Luciferic Past and Ahrimanic Future
CW 194	The Mission of Michael. The Revelation of the Actual Mysteries of the Human Being
CW 195	Cosmic New Year and the New Year Idea
CW 196	Spiritual and Social Transformations in the Development of Humanity
CW 197	Polarities in the Development of Humanity: West and East Materialism and Mysticism Knowledge and Belief
CW 198	Healing Factors for the Social Organism
CW 199	Spiritual Science as Knowledge of the Foundational Impulses of Social Formation

148 ✻ Conscious Society

CW 200	The New Spirituality and the Christ-Experience of the 20th Century
CW 201	The Correspondences Between Microcosm and Macrocosm. The Human Being—A Hieroglyph of the Universe. The Human Being in Relationship with the Cosmos: 1
CW 202	The Bridge between the World-Spirituality and the Physical Aspect of the Human Being. The Search for the New Isis, the Divine Sophia. The Human Being in Relationship with the Cosmos: 2
CW 203	The Responsibility of Human Beings for the Development of the World through their Spiritual Connection with the Planet Earth and the World of the Stars. The Human Being in Relationship with the Cosmos: 3
CW 204	Perspectives of the Development of Humanity. The Materialistic Knowledge-Impulse and the Task of Anthroposophy. The Human Being in Relationship with the Cosmos: 4
CW 205	Human Development, World-Soul, and World-Spirit. Part One: The Human Being as a Being of Body and Soul in Relationship to the World. The Human Being in Relationship with the Cosmos: 5
CW 206	Human Development, World-Soul, and World-Spirit. Part Two: The Human Being as a Spiritual Being in the Process of Historical Development. The Human Being in Relationship with the Cosmos: 6
CW 207	Anthroposophy as Cosmosophy. Part One: Characteristic Features of the Human Being in the Earthly and the Cosmic Realms. The Human Being in Relationship with the Cosmos: 7
CW 208	Anthroposophy as Cosmosophy. Part Two: The Forming of the Human Being as the Result of Cosmic Influence. The Human Being in Relationship with the Cosmos: 8
CW 209	Nordic and Central European Spiritual Impulses. The Festival of the Appearance of Christ. The Human Being in Relationship with the Cosmos: 9
CW 210	Old and New Methods of Initiation. Drama and Poetry in the Change of Consciousness in the Modern Age
CW 211	The Sun Mystery and the Mystery of Death and Resurrection. Exoteric and Esoteric Christianity
CW 212	Human Soul Life and Spiritual Striving in Connection with World and Earth Development
CW 213	Human Questions and World Answers
CW 214	The Mystery of the Trinity: The Human Being in Relationship with the Spiritual World in the Course of Time
CW 215	Philosophy, Cosmology, and Religion in Anthroposophy
CW 216	The Fundamental Impulses of the World-Historical Development of Humanity
CW 217	Spiritually Active Forces in the Coexistence of the Older and Younger Generations. Pedagogical Course for Youth

Rudolf Steiner's Collected Works * 149

CW 217a	Youth's Cognitive Task
CW 218	Spiritual Connections in the Forming of the Human Organism
CW 219	The Relationship of the World of the Stars to the Human Being, and of the Human Being to the World of the Stars. The Spiritual Communion of Humanity
CW 220	Living Knowledge of Nature. Intellectual Fall and Spiritual Redemption
CW 221	Earth-Knowing and Heaven-Insight
CW 222	The Imparting of Impulses to World-Historical Events through Spiritual Powers
CW 223	The Cycle of the Year as Breathing Process of the Earth and the Four Great Festival-Seasons. Anthroposophy and the Human Heart (Gemüt)
CW 224	The Human Soul and its Connection with Divine-Spiritual Individualities. The Internalization of the Festivals of the Year
CW 225	Three Perspectives of Anthroposophy. Cultural Phenomena observed from a Spiritual-Scientific Perspective
CW 226	Human Being, Human Destiny, and World Development
CW 227	Initiation-Knowledge
CW 228	Science of Initiation and Knowledge of the Stars. The Human Being in the Past, the Present, and the Future from the Viewpoint of the Development of Consciousness
CW 229	The Experiencing of the Course of the Year in Four Cosmic Imaginations
CW 230	The Human Being as Harmony of the Creative, Building, and Formative World-Word
CW 231	The Supersensible Human Being, Understood Anthroposophically
CW 232	The Forming of the Mysteries
CW 233	World History Illuminated by Anthroposophy and as the Foundation for Knowledge of the Human Spirit
CW 233a	Mystery Sites of the Middle Ages: Rosicrucianism and the Modern Initiation-Principle. The Festival of Easter as Part of the History of the Mysteries of Humanity
CW 234	Anthroposophy. A Summary after 21 Years
CW 235	Esoteric Observations of Karmic Relationships in 6 Volumes, Vol. 1
CW 236	Esoteric Observations of Karmic Relationships in 6 Volumes, Vol. 2
CW 237	Esoteric Observations of Karmic Relationships in 6 Volumes, Vol. 3: The Karmic Relationships of the Anthroposophical Movement
CW 238	Esoteric Observations of Karmic Relationships in 6 Volumes, Vol. 4: The Spiritual Life of the Present in Relationship to the Anthroposophical Movement
CW 239	Esoteric Observations of Karmic Relationships in 6 Volumes, Vol. 5

CW 240	Esoteric Observations of Karmic Relationships in 6 Volumes, Vol. 6
CW 243	The Consciousness of the Initiate
CW 245	Instructions for an Esoteric Schooling
CW 250	The Building-Up of the Anthroposophical Society. From the Beginning to the Outbreak of the First World War
CW 251	The History of the Goetheanum Building-Association
CW 252	Life in the Anthroposophical Society from the First World War to the Burning of the First Goetheanum
CW 253	The Problems of Living Together in the Anthroposophical Society. On the Dornach Crisis of 1915. With Highlights on Swedenborg's Clairvoyance, the Views of Freudian Psychoanalysts, and the Concept of Love in Relation to Mysticism
CW 254	The Occult Movement in the 19th Century and Its Relationship to World Culture. Significant Points from the Exoteric Cultural Life around the Middle of the 19th Century
CW 255	Rudolf Steiner during the First World War
CW 255a	Anthroposophy and the Reformation of Society. On the History of the Threefold Movement
CW 255b	Anthroposophy and Its Opponents, 1919–1921
CW 256	How Can the Anthroposophical Movement Be Financed?
CW 256a	Futurum, Inc. / International Laboratories, Inc.
CW 256b	The Coming Day, Inc.
CW 257	Anthroposophical Community-Building
CW 258	The History of and Conditions for the Anthroposophical Movement in Relationship to the Anthroposophical Society. A Stimulus to Self-Contemplation
CW 259	The Year of Destiny 1923 in the History of the Anthroposophical Society. From the Burning of the Goetheanum to the Christmas Conference
CW 260	The Christmas Conference for the Founding of the General Anthroposophical Society
CW 260a	The Constitution of the General Anthroposophical Society and the School for Spiritual Science. The Rebuilding of the Goetheanum
CW 261	Our Dead. Addresses, Words of Remembrance, and Meditative Verses, 1906–1924
CW 262	Rudolf Steiner and Marie Steiner-von Sivers: Correspondence and Documents, 1901–1925
CW 263/1	Rudolf Steiner and Edith Maryon: Correspondence: Letters, Verses, Sketches, 1912–1924
CW 264	On the History and the Contents of the First Section of the Esoteric School from 1904 to 1914. Letters, Newsletters, Documents, Lectures
CW 265	On the History and from the Contents of the Ritual-Knowledge Section of the Esoteric School from 1904 to 1914. Documents, and Lectures from the Years 1906 to 1914, as well as on New Approaches to Ritual-Knowledge Work in the Years 1921–1924

Rudolf Steiner's Collected Works * 151

CW 266/1	From the Contents of the Esoteric Lessons. Volume 1: 1904–1909. Notes from Memory of Participants. Meditation texts from the notes of Rudolf Steiner
CW 266/2	From the Contents of the Esoteric Lessons. Volume 2: 1910–1912. Notes from Memory of Participants
CW 266/3	From the Contents of the Esoteric Lessons. Volume 3: 1913, 1914 and 1920–1923. Notes from Memory of Participants. Meditation texts from the notes of Rudolf Steiner
CW 267	Soul-Exercises: Vol. 1: Exercises with Word and Image Meditations for the Methodological Development of Higher Powers of Knowledge, 1904–1924
CW 268	Soul-Exercises: Vol. 2: Mantric Verses, 1903–1925
CW 269	Ritual Texts for the Celebration of the Free Christian Religious Instruction. The Collected Verses for Teachers and Students of the Waldorf School
CW 270	Esoteric Instructions for the First Class of the School for Spiritual Science at the Goetheanum 1924, 4 Volumes
CW 271	Art and Knowledge of Art. Foundations of a New Aesthetic
CW 272	Spiritual-Scientific Commentary on Goethe's 'Faust' in Two Volumes. Vol. 1: Faust, the Striving Human Being
CW 273	Spiritual-Scientific Commentary on Goethe's 'Faust' in Two Volumes. Vol. 2: The Faust-Problem
CW 274	Addresses for the Christmas Plays from the Old Folk Traditions
CW 275	Art in the Light of Mystery-Wisdom
CW 276	The Artistic in Its Mission in the World. The Genius of Language. The World of Self-Revealing Radiant Appearances—Anthroposophy and Art. Anthroposophy and Poetry
CW 277	Eurythmy. The Revelation of the Speaking Soul
CW 277a	The Origin and Development of Eurythmy
CW 278	Eurythmy as Visible Song
CW 279	Eurythmy as Visible Speech
CW 280	The Method and Nature of Speech Formation
CW 281	The Art of Recitation and Declamation
CW 282	Speech Formation and Dramatic Art
CW 283	The Nature of Things Musical and the Experience of Tone in the Human Being
CW 284/285	Images of Occult Seals and Pillars. The Munich Congress of Whitsun 1907 and Its Consequences
CW 286	Paths to a New Style of Architecture. 'And the Building Becomes Human'
CW 287	The Building at Dornach as a Symbol of Historical Becoming and an Artistic Transformation Impulse
CW 288	Style-Forms in the Living Organic
CW 289	The Building-Idea of the Goetheanum: Lectures with Slides from the Years 1920–1921
CW 290	The Building-Idea of the Goetheanum: Lectures with Slides from the Years 1920–1921

CW 291	The Nature of Colours
CW 291a	Knowledge of Colours. Supplementary Volume to 'The Nature of Colours'
CW 292	Art History as Image of Inner Spiritual Impulses
CW 293	General Knowledge of the Human Being as the Foundation of Pedagogy
CW 294	The Art of Education, Methodology and Didactics
CW 295	The Art of Education: Seminar Discussions and Lectures on Lesson Planning
CW 296	The Question of Education as a Social Question
CW 297	The Idea and Practice of the Waldorf School
CW 297a	Education for Life: Self-Education and the Practice of Pedagogy
CW 298	Rudolf Steiner in the Waldorf School
CW 299	Spiritual-Scientific Observations on Speech
CW 300a	Conferences with the Teachers of the Free Waldorf School in Stuttgart, 1919 to 1924, in 3 Volumes, Vol. 1
CW 300b	Conferences with the Teachers of the Free Waldorf School in Stuttgart, 1919 to 1924, in 3 Volumes, Vol. 2
CW 300c	Conferences with the Teachers of the Free Waldorf School in Stuttgart, 1919 to 1924, in 3 Volumes, Vol. 3
CW 301	The Renewal of Pedagogical-Didactical Art through Spiritual Science
CW 302	Knowledge of the Human Being and the Forming of Class Lessons
CW 302a	Education and Teaching from a Knowledge of the Human Being
CW 303	The Healthy Development of the Human Being
CW 304	Methods of Education and Teaching Based on Anthroposophy
CW 304a	Anthroposophical Knowledge of the Human Being and Pedagogy
CW 305	The Soul-Spiritual Foundational Forces of the Art of Education. Spiritual Values in Education and Social Life
CW 306	Pedagogical Praxis from the Viewpoint of a Spiritual-Scientific Knowledge of the Human Being. The Education of the Child and Young Human Beings
CW 307	The Spiritual Life of the Present and Education
CW 308	The Method of Teaching and the Life-Requirements for Teaching
CW 309	Anthroposophical Pedagogy and Its Prerequisites
CW 310	The Pedagogical Value of a Knowledge of the Human Being and the Cultural Value of Pedagogy
CW 311	The Art of Education from an Understanding of the Being of Humanity
CW 312	Spiritual Science and Medicine
CW 313	Spiritual-Scientific Viewpoints on Therapy
CW 314	Physiology and Therapy Based on Spiritual Science
CW 315	Curative Eurythmy
CW 316	Meditative Observations and Instructions for a Deepening of the Art of Healing
CW 317	The Curative Education Course

CW 318	The Working Together of Doctors and Pastors
CW 319	Anthroposophical Knowledge of the Human Being and Medicine
CW 320	Spiritual-Scientific Impulses for the Development of Physics 1: The First Natural-Scientific Course: Light, Colour, Tone, Mass, Electricity, Magnetism
CW 321	Spiritual-Scientific Impulses for the Development of Physics 2: The Second Natural-Scientific Course: Warmth at the Border of Positive and Negative Materiality
CW 322	The Borders of the Knowledge of Nature
CW 323	The Relationship of the various Natural-Scientific Fields to Astronomy
CW 324	Nature Observation, Mathematics, and Scientific Experimentation and Results from the Viewpoint of Anthroposophy
CW 324a	The Fourth Dimension in Mathematics and Reality
CW 325	Natural Science and the World-Historical Development of Humanity since Ancient Times
CW 326	The Moment of the Coming Into Being of Natural Science in World History and Its Development Since Then
CW 327	Spiritual-Scientific Foundations for Success in Farming. The Agricultural Course
CW 328	The Social Question
CW 329	The Liberation of the Human Being as the Foundation for a New Social Form
CW 330	The Renewal of the Social Organism
CW 331	Work-Council and Socialization
CW 332	The Alliance for Threefolding and the Total Reform of Society. The Council on Culture and the Liberation of the Spiritual Life
CW 332a	The Social Future
CW 333	Freedom of Thought and Social Forces
CW 334	From the Unified State to the Threefold Social Organism
CW 335	The Crisis of the Present and the Path to Healthy Thinking
CW 336	The Great Questions of the Times and Anthroposophical Spiritual Knowledge
CW 337a	Social Ideas, Social Reality, Social Practice, Vol. 1: Question-and-Answer Evenings and Study Evenings of the Alliance for the Threefold Social Organism in Stuttgart, 1919–1920
CW 337b	Social Ideas, Social Realities, Social Practice, Vol. 2: Discussion Evenings of the Swiss Alliance for the Threefold Social Organism
CW 338	How Does One Work on Behalf of the Impulse for the Threefold Social Organism?
CW 339	Anthroposophy, Threefold Social Organism, and the Art of Public Speaking
CW 340	The National-Economics Course. The Tasks of a New Science of Economics, Volume 1
CW 341	The National-Economics Seminar. The Tasks of a New Science of Economics, Volume 2

CW 342   Lectures and Courses on Christian Religious Work, Vol. 1: Anthroposophical Foundations for a Renewed Christian Religious Working
CW 343   Lectures and Courses on Christian Religious Work, Vol. 2: Spiritual Knowledge—Religious Feeling—Cultic Doing
CW 344   Lectures and Courses on Christian Religious Work, Vol. 3: Lectures at the Founding of the Christian Community
CW 345   Lectures and Courses on Christian Religious Work, Vol. 4: Concerning the Nature of the Working Word
CW 346   Lectures and Courses on Christian Religious Work, Vol. 5: The Apocalypse and the Work of the Priest
CW 347   The Knowledge of the Nature of the Human Being According to Body, Soul and Spirit. On Earlier Conditions of the Earth
CW 348   On Health and Illness. Foundations of a Spiritual-Scientific Doctrine of the Senses
CW 349   On the Life of the Human Being and of the Earth. On the Nature of Christianity
CW 350   Rhythms in the Cosmos and in the Human Being. How Does One Come To See the Spiritual World?
CW 351   The Human Being and the World. The Influence of the Spirit in Nature. On the Nature of Bees
CW 352   Nature and the Human Being Observed Spiritual-Scientifically
CW 353   The History of Humanity and the World-Views of the Folk Cultures
CW 354   The Creation of the World and the Human Being. Life on Earth and the Influence of the Stars

SIGNIFICANT EVENTS IN THE LIFE OF RUDOLF STEINER

1829: June 23: birth of Johann Steiner (1829–1910)—Rudolf Steiner's father—in Geras, Lower Austria.
1834: May 8: birth of Franciska Blie (1834–1918)—Rudolf Steiner's mother—in Horn, Lower Austria. 'My father and mother were both children of the glorious Lower Austrian forest district north of the Danube.'
1860: May 16: marriage of Johann Steiner and Franciska Blie.
1861: February 25: birth of *Rudolf Joseph Lorenz Steiner* in Kraljevec, Croatia, near the border with Hungary, where Johann Steiner works as a telegrapher for the South Austria Railroad. Rudolf Steiner is baptized two days later, February 27, the date usually given as his birthday.
1862: Summer: the family moves to Mödling, Lower Austria.
1863: The family moves to Pottschach, Lower Austria, near the Styrian border, where Johann Steiner becomes stationmaster. 'The view stretched to the mountains ... majestic peaks in the distance and the sweet charm of nature in the immediate surroundings.'
1864: November 15: birth of Rudolf Steiner's sister, Leopoldine (d. November 1, 1927). She will become a seamstress and live with her parents for the rest of her life.
1866: July 28: birth of Rudolf Steiner's deaf-mute brother, Gustav (d. May 1, 1941).
1867: Rudolf Steiner enters the village school. Following a disagreement between his father and the schoolmaster, whose wife falsely accused the boy of causing a commotion, Rudolf Steiner is taken out of school and taught at home.
1868: A critical experience. Unknown to the family, an aunt dies in a distant town. Sitting in the station waiting room, Rudolf Steiner sees her 'form,' which speaks to him, asking for help. 'Beginning with this experience, a new soul life began in the boy, one in which not only the outer trees and mountains spoke to him, but also the worlds that lay behind them. From this moment on, the boy began to live with the spirits of nature...'
1869: The family moves to the peaceful, rural village of Neudörfl, near Wiener-Neustadt in present-day Austria. Rudolf Steiner attends the village school. Because of the 'unorthodoxy' of his writing and spelling, he has to do 'extra lessons.'
1870: Through a book lent to him by his tutor, he discovers geometry: 'To grasp something purely in the spirit brought me inner happiness. I know that I first learned happiness through geometry.' The same tutor allows

him to draw, while other students still struggle with their reading and writing. 'An artistic element' thus enters his education.

1871: Though his parents are not religious, Rudolf Steiner becomes a 'church child,' a favourite of the priest, who was 'an exceptional character.' 'Up to the age of ten or eleven, among those I came to know, he was far and away the most significant.' Among other things, he introduces Steiner to Copernican, heliocentric cosmology. As an altar boy, Rudolf Steiner serves at Masses, funerals, and Corpus Christi processions. At year's end, after an incident in which he escapes a thrashing, his father forbids him to go to church.

1872: Rudolf Steiner transfers to grammar school in Wiener-Neustadt, a five-mile walk from home, which must be done in all weathers.

1873–75: Through his teachers and on his own, Rudolf Steiner has many wonderful experiences with science and mathematics. Outside school, he teaches himself analytic geometry, trigonometry, differential equations, and calculus.

1876: Rudolf Steiner begins tutoring other students. He learns bookbinding from his father. He also teaches himself stenography.

1877: Rudolf Steiner discovers Kant's *Critique of Pure Reason*, which he reads and rereads. He also discovers and reads von Rotteck's *World History*.

1878: He studies extensively in contemporary psychology and philosophy.

1879: Rudolf Steiner graduates from high school with honours. His father is transferred to Inzersdorf, near Vienna. He uses his first visit to Vienna 'to purchase a great number of philosophy books'—Kant, Fichte, Schelling, and Hegel, as well as numerous histories of philosophy. His aim: to find a path from the 'I' to nature.

October 1879–1883: Rudolf Steiner attends the Technical College in Vienna—to study mathematics, chemistry, physics, mineralogy, botany, zoology, biology, geology, and mechanics—with a scholarship. He also attends lectures in history and literature, while avidly reading philosophy on his own. His two favourite professors are Karl Julius Schröer (German language and literature) and Edmund Reitlinger (physics). He also audits lectures by Robert Zimmermann on aesthetics and Franz Brentano on philosophy. During this year he begins his friendship with Moritz Zitter (1861–1921), who will help support him financially when he is in Berlin.

1880: Rudolf Steiner attends lectures on Schiller and Goethe by Karl Julius Schröer, who becomes his mentor. Also 'through a remarkable combination of circumstances,' he meets Felix Koguzki, a 'herb gatherer' and healer, who could 'see deeply into the secrets of nature.' Rudolf Steiner will meet and study with this 'emissary of the Master' throughout his time in Vienna.

1881: January: '… I didn't sleep a wink. I was busy with philosophical problems until about 12:30 a.m. Then, finally, I threw myself down on my couch. All my striving during the previous year had been to research whether the following statement by Schelling was true or not: *Within everyone dwells a secret, marvelous capacity to draw back from the stream of time—out of the self clothed in all that comes to us from outside—into our innermost being and there, in the immutable form of the Eternal, to look into ourselves.* I believe, and I am still quite certain of it, that I discovered this capacity in myself; I had long had an inkling of it. Now the whole of idealist philosophy stood before me in modified form. What's a sleepless night compared to that!'

Rudolf Steiner begins communicating with leading thinkers of the day, who send him books in return, which he reads eagerly.

July: 'I am not one of those who dives into the day like an animal in human form. I pursue a quite specific goal, an idealistic aim—knowledge of the truth! This cannot be done offhandedly. It requires the greatest striving in the world, free of all egotism, and equally of all resignation.'

August: Steiner puts down on paper for the first time thoughts for a 'Philosophy of Freedom.' 'The striving for the absolute: this human yearning is freedom.' He also seeks to outline a 'peasant philosophy,' describing what the worldview of a 'peasant'—one who lives close to the earth and the old ways—really is.

1881–1882: Felix Koguzki, the herb gatherer, reveals himself to be the envoy of another, higher initiatory personality, who instructs Rudolf Steiner to penetrate Fichte's philosophy and to master modern scientific thinking as a preparation for right entry into the spirit. This 'Master' also teaches him the double (evolutionary and involutionary) nature of time.

1882: Through the offices of Karl Julius Schröer, Rudolf Steiner is asked by Joseph Kürschner to edit Goethe's scientific works for the *Deutschen National-Literatur* edition. He writes 'A Possible Critique of Atomistic Concepts' and sends it to Friedrich Theodor Vischer.

1883: Rudolf Steiner completes his college studies and begins work on the Goethe project.

1884: First volume of Goethe's *Scientific Writings* (CW 1) appears (March). He lectures on Goethe and Lessing, and Goethe's approach to science. In July, he enters the household of Ladislaus and Pauline Specht as tutor to the four Specht boys. He will live there until 1890. At this time, he meets Josef Breuer (1842–1925), the co-author with Sigmund Freud of *Studies in Hysteria*, who is the Specht family doctor.

1885: While continuing to edit Goethe's writings, Rudolf Steiner reads deeply in contemporary philosophy (Eduard von Hartmann, Johannes Volkelt, and Richard Wahle, among others).

1886: May: Rudolf Steiner sends Kürschner the manuscript of *Outlines of Goethe's Theory of Knowledge* (CW 2), which appears in October, and which he sends out widely. He also meets the poet Marie Eugenie Delle Grazie and writes 'Nature and Our Ideals' for her. He attends her salon, where he meets many priests, theologians, and philosophers, who will become his friends. Meanwhile, the director of the Goethe Archive in Weimar requests his collaboration with the *Sophien* edition of Goethe's works, particularly the writings on colour.

1887: At the beginning of the year, Rudolf Steiner is very sick. As the year progresses and his health improves, he becomes increasingly 'a man of letters,' lecturing, writing essays, and taking part in Austrian cultural life. In August–September, the second volume of Goethe's *Scientific Writings* appears.

1888: January–July: Rudolf Steiner assumes editorship of the 'German Weekly' (*Deutsche Wochenschrift*). He begins lecturing more intensively, giving, for example, a lecture titled 'Goethe as Father of a New Aesthetics.' He meets and becomes soul friends with Friedrich Eckstein (1861–1939), a vegetarian, philosopher of symbolism, alchemist, and musician, who will introduce him to various spiritual currents (including Theosophy) and with whom he will meditate and interpret esoteric and alchemical texts.

1889: Rudolf Steiner first reads Nietzsche (*Beyond Good and Evil*). He encounters Theosophy again and learns of Madame Blavatsky in the Theosophical circle around Marie Lang (1858–1934). Here he also meets well-known figures of Austrian life, as well as esoteric figures like the occultist Franz Hartmann and Karl Leinigen-Billigen (translator of C.G. Harrison's *The Transcendental Universe*). During this period, Steiner first reads A.P. Sinnett's *Esoteric Buddhism* and Mabel Collins's *Light on the Path*. He also begins travelling, visiting Budapest, Weimar, and Berlin (where he meets philosopher Eduard von Hartmann).

1890: Rudolf Steiner finishes volume 3 of Goethe's scientific writings. He begins his doctoral dissertation, which will become *Truth and Science* (CW 3). He also meets the poet and feminist Rosa Mayreder (1858–1938), with whom he can exchange his most intimate thoughts. In September, Rudolf Steiner moves to Weimar to work in the Goethe-Schiller Archive.

1891: Volume 3 of the Kürschner edition of Goethe appears. Meanwhile, Rudolf Steiner edits Goethe's studies in mineralogy and scientific writings for the *Sophien* edition. He meets Ludwig Laistner of the Cotta Publishing Company, who asks for a book on the basic question of metaphysics. From this will result, ultimately, *The Philosophy of Freedom* (CW 4), which will be published not by Cotta but by Emil Felber. In October, Rudolf Steiner takes the oral exam for a doctorate in philosophy, mathematics, and mechanics at Rostock University, receiving his doctorate on the twenty-sixth. In November, he gives his first lecture on Goethe's 'Fairy Tale' in Vienna.

1892: Rudolf Steiner continues work at the Goethe-Schiller Archive and on his *Philosophy of Freedom*. *Truth and Science*, his doctoral dissertation, is published. Steiner undertakes to write introductions to books on Schopenhauer and Jean Paul for Cotta. At year's end, he finds lodging with Anna Eunike, née Schulz (1853–1911), a widow with four daughters and a son. He also develops a friendship with Otto Erich Hartleben (1864–1905) with whom he shares literary interests.

1893: Rudolf Steiner begins his habit of producing many reviews and articles. In March, he gives a lecture titled 'Hypnotism, with Reference to Spiritism.' In September, volume 4 of the Kürschner edition is completed. In November, *The Philosophy of Freedom* appears. This year, too, he meets John Henry Mackay (1864–1933), the anarchist and Max Stirner scholar.

1894: Rudolf Steiner meets Elisabeth Förster Nietzsche, the philosopher's sister, and begins to read Nietzsche in earnest, beginning with the as yet unpublished *Antichrist*. He also meets Ernst Haeckel (1834–1919). In the fall, he begins to write *Nietzsche, A Fighter against His Time* (CW 5).

1895: May, *Nietzsche, A Fighter against His Time* appears.

1896: January 22: Rudolf Steiner sees Friedrich Nietzsche for the first and only time. Moves between the Nietzsche and the Goethe-Schiller Archives, where he completes his work before year's end. He falls out with Elisabeth Förster Nietzsche, thus ending his association with the Nietzsche Archive.

1897: Rudolf Steiner finishes the manuscript of *Goethe's Worldview* (CW 6). He moves to Berlin with Anna Eunike and begins editorship of the *Magazin für Literatur*. From now on, Steiner will write countless reviews, literary and philosophical articles, and so on. He begins lecturing at the 'Free Literary Society.' In September, he attends the Zionist Congress in Basel. He sides with Dreyfus in the Dreyfus affair.

1898: Rudolf Steiner is very active as an editor in the political, artistic, and theatrical life of Berlin. He becomes friendly with John Henry Mackay and poet Ludwig Jacobowski (1868–1900). He joins Jacobowski's circle of writers, artists, and scientists—'The Coming Ones' (*Die Kommenden*)— and contributes lectures to the group until 1903. He also lectures at the 'League for College Pedagogy.' He writes an article for Goethe's sesquicentennial, 'Goethe's Secret Revelation,' on the 'Fairy Tale of the Green Snake and the Beautiful Lily.'

1898–99: 'This was a trying time for my soul as I looked at Christianity. . . . I was able to progress only by contemplating, by means of spiritual perception, the evolution of Christianity. . . . Conscious knowledge of real Christianity began to dawn in me around the turn of the century. This seed continued to develop. My soul trial occurred shortly before the beginning of the twentieth century. It was decisive for my soul's development that I stood spiritually before the Mystery of Golgotha in a deep and solemn celebration of knowledge.'

1899: Rudolf Steiner begins teaching and giving lectures and lecture cycles at the Workers' College, founded by Wilhelm Liebknecht (1826–1900). He will continue to do so until 1904. Writes: *Literature and Spiritual Life in the Nineteenth Century; Individualism in Philosophy*; *Haeckel and His Opponents; Poetry in the Present;* and begins what will become (fifteen years later) *The Riddles of Philosophy* (CW 18). He also meets many artists and writers, including Käthe Kollwitz, Stefan Zweig, and Rainer Maria Rilke. On October 31, he marries Anna Eunike.

1900: 'I thought that the turn of the century must bring humanity a new light. It seemed to me that the separation of human thinking and willing from the spirit had peaked. A turn or reversal of direction in human evolution seemed to me a necessity.' Rudolf Steiner finishes *World and Life Views in the Nineteenth Century* (the second part of what will become *The Riddles of Philosophy*) and dedicates it to Ernst Haeckel. It is published in March. He continues lecturing at *Die Kommenden*, whose leadership he assumes after the death of Jacobowski. Also, he gives the Gutenberg Jubilee lecture before 7,000 typesetters and printers. In September, Rudolf Steiner is invited by Count and Countess Brockdorff to lecture in the Theosophical Library. His first lecture is on Nietzsche. His second lecture is titled 'Goethe's Secret Revelation.' October 6, he begins a lecture cycle on the mystics that will become *Mystics after Modernism* (CW 7). November-December: 'Marie von Sivers appears in the audience....' Also in November, Steiner gives his first lecture at the Giordano Bruno Bund (where he will continue to lecture until May, 1905). He speaks on Bruno and modern Rome, focusing on the importance of the philosophy of Thomas Aquinas as monism.

1901: In continual financial straits, Rudolf Steiner's early friends Moritz Zitter and Rosa Mayreder help support him. In October, he begins the lecture cycle *Christianity as Mystical Fact* (CW 8) at the Theosophical Library. In November, he gives his first 'Theosophical lecture' on Goethe's 'Fairy Tale' in Hamburg at the invitation of Wilhelm Hubbe-Schleiden. He also attends a gathering to celebrate the founding of the Theosophical Society at Count and Countess Brockdorff's. He gives a lecture cycle, 'From Buddha to Christ,' for the circle of the *Kommenden*. November 17, Marie von Sivers asks Rudolf Steiner if Theosophy needs a Western-Christian spiritual movement (to complement Theosophy's Eastern emphasis). 'The question was posed. Now, following spiritual laws, I could begin to give an answer....' In December, Rudolf Steiner writes his first article for a Theosophical publication. At year's end, the Brockdorffs and possibly Wilhelm Hubbe-Schleiden ask Rudolf Steiner to join the Theosophical Society and undertake the leadership of the German section. Rudolf Steiner agrees, on the condition that Marie von Sivers (then in Italy) work with him.

1902: Beginning in January, Rudolf Steiner attends the opening of the Workers' School in Spandau with Rosa Luxemberg (1870–1919). January 17, Rudolf Steiner joins the Theosophical Society. In April, he is asked to become general secretary of the German Section of the Theosophical Society, and works on preparations for its founding. In July, he visits London for a Theosophical congress. He meets Bertram Keightly, G.R.S. Mead, A.P. Sinnett, and Annie Besant, among others. In September, *Christianity as Mystical Fact* appears. In October, Rudolf Steiner gives his first public lecture on Theosophy ('Monism and Theosophy') to about three hundred people at the Giordano Bruno Bund. On October 19–21, the German Section of the Theosophical Society has its first meeting; Rudolf Steiner is the general secretary, and Annie Besant attends. Steiner lectures on practical karma studies. On October 23, Annie Besant inducts Rudolf Steiner into the Esoteric School of the Theosophical Society. On October 25, Steiner begins a weekly series of lectures: 'The Field of Theosophy.' During this year, Rudolf Steiner also first meets Ita Wegman (1876–1943), who will become his close collaborator in his final years.

1903: Rudolf Steiner holds about 300 lectures and seminars. In May, the first issue of the periodical *Luzifer* appears. In June, Rudolf Steiner visits

London for the first meeting of the Federation of the European Sections of the Theosophical Society, where he meets Colonel Olcott. He begins to write *Theosophy* (CW 9).

1904: Rudolf Steiner continues lecturing at the Workers' College and elsewhere (about 90 lectures), while lecturing intensively all over Germany among Theosophists (about 140 lectures). In February, he meets Carl Unger (1878–1929), who will become a member of the board of the Anthroposophical Society (1913). In March, he meets Michael Bauer (1871–1929), a Christian mystic, who will also be on the board. In May, *Theosophy* appears, with the dedication: 'To the spirit of Giordano Bruno.' Rudolf Steiner and Marie von Sivers visit London for meetings with Annie Besant. June: Rudolf Steiner and Marie von Sivers attend the meeting of the Federation of European Sections of the Theosophical Society in Amsterdam. In July, Steiner begins the articles in *Luzifer-Gnosis* that will become *How to Know Higher Worlds* (CW 10) and *Cosmic Memory* (CW 11). In September, Annie Besant visits Germany. In December, Steiner lectures on Freemasonry. He mentions the High Grade Masonry derived from John Yarker and represented by Theodore Reuss and Karl Kellner as a blank slate 'into which a good image could be placed.'

1905: This year, Steiner ends his non-Theosophical lecturing activity. Supported by Marie von Sivers, his Theosophical lecturing—both in public and in the Theosophical Society—increases significantly: 'The German Theosophical Movement is of exceptional importance.' Steiner recommends reading, among others, Fichte, Jacob Boehme, and Angelus Silesius. He begins to introduce Christian themes into Theosophy. He also begins to work with doctors (Felix Peipers and Ludwig Noll). In July, he is in London for the Federation of European Sections, where he attends a lecture by Annie Besant: 'I have seldom seen Mrs. Besant speak in so inward and heartfelt a manner....' 'Through Mrs. Besant I have found the way to H.P. Blavatsky.' September to October, he gives a course of thirty-one lectures for a small group of esoteric students. In October, the annual meeting of the German Section of the Theosophical Society, which still remains very small, takes place. Rudolf Steiner reports membership has risen from 121 to 377 members. In November, seeking to establish esoteric 'continuity,' Rudolf Steiner and Marie von Sivers participate in a 'Memphis-Misraim' Masonic ceremony. They pay forty-five marks for membership. 'Yesterday, you saw how little remains of former esoteric institutions.' 'We are dealing only with a "framework"... for the present, nothing lies behind it. The occult powers have completely withdrawn.'

1906: Expansion of Theosophical work. Rudolf Steiner gives about 245 lectures, only 44 of which take place in Berlin. Cycles are given in Paris, Leipzig, Stuttgart, and Munich. Esoteric work also intensifies. Rudolf Steiner begins writing *An Outline of Esoteric Science* (CW 13). In January, Rudolf Steiner receives permission (a patent) from the Great Orient of the Scottish A & A Thirty-Three Degree Rite of the Order of the Ancient

Freemasons of the Memphis-Misraim Rite to direct a chapter under the name 'Mystica Aeterna.' This will become the 'Cognitive-Ritual Section' (also called 'Misraim Service') of the Esoteric School. (See: *Freemasonry and Ritual Work: The Misraim Service*, CW 265). During this time, Steiner also meets Albert Schweitzer. In May, he is in Paris, where he visits Edouard Schuré. Many Russians attend his lectures (including Konstantin Balmont, Dimitri Mereszkovski, Zinaida Hippius, and Maximilian Woloshin). He attends the General Meeting of the European Federation of the Theosophical Society, at which Col. Olcott is present for the last time. He spends the year's end in Venice and Rome, where he writes and works on his translation of H.P. Blavatsky's *Key to Theosophy*.

1907: Further expansion of the German Theosophical Movement according to the Rosicrucian directive to 'introduce spirit into the world'—in education, in social questions, in art, and in science. In February, Col. Olcott dies in Adyar. Before he dies, Olcott indicates that 'the Masters' wish Annie Besant to succeed him: much politicking ensues. Rudolf Steiner supports Besant's candidacy. April-May: preparations for the Congress of the Federation of European Sections of the Theosophical Society—the great, watershed Whitsun 'Munich Congress,' attended by Annie Besant and others. Steiner decides to separate Eastern and Western (Christian-Rosicrucian) esoteric schools. He takes his esoteric school out of the Theosophical Society (Besant and Rudolf Steiner are 'in harmony' on this). Steiner makes his first lecture tours to Austria and Hungary. That summer, he is in Italy. In September, he visits Edouard Schuré, who will write the introduction to the French edition of *Christianity as Mystical Fact* in Barr, Alsace. Rudolf Steiner writes the autobiographical statement known as the 'Barr Document.' In *Luzifer-Gnosis*, 'The Education of the Child' appears.

1908: The movement grows (membership: 1,150). Lecturing expands. Steiner makes his first extended lecture tour to Holland and Scandinavia, as well as visits to Naples and Sicily. Themes: St. John's Gospel, the Apocalypse, Egypt, science, philosophy, and logic. *Luzifer-Gnosis* ceases publication. In Berlin, Marie von Sivers (with Johanna Mücke (1864–1949) forms the *Philosophisch-Theosophisch* (after 1915 *Philosophisch-Anthroposophisch*) *Verlag* to publish Steiner's work. Steiner gives lecture cycles titled *The Gospel of St. John* (CW 103) and *The Apocalypse* (104).

1909: *An Outline of Esoteric Science* appears. Lecturing and travel continues. Rudolf Steiner's spiritual research expands to include the polarity of Lucifer and Ahriman; the work of great individualities in history; the Maitreya Buddha and the Bodhisattvas; spiritual economy (CW 109); the work of the spiritual hierarchies in heaven and on earth (CW 110). He also deepens and intensifies his research into the Gospels, giving lectures on the Gospel of St. Luke (CW 114) with the first mention of two Jesus children. Meets and becomes friends with Christian Morgenstern (1871–1914). In April, he lays the foundation stone for the Malsch model—the building that will lead to the first Goetheanum. In May, the International Congress of the Federation of European Sections of the

Theosophical Society takes place in Budapest. Rudolf Steiner receives the Subba Row medal for *How to Know Higher Worlds*. During this time, Charles W. Leadbeater discovers Jiddu Krishnamurti (1895–1986) and proclaims him the future 'world teacher,' the bearer of the Maitreya Buddha and the 'reappearing Christ.' In October, Steiner delivers seminal lectures on 'anthroposophy,' which he will try, unsuccessfully, to rework over the next years into the unfinished work, *Anthroposophy (A Fragment)* (CW 45).

1910: New themes: *The Reappearance of Christ in the Etheric* (CW 118); *The Fifth Gospel; The Mission of Folk Souls* (CW 121); *Occult History* (CW 126); the evolving development of etheric cognitive capacities. Rudolf Steiner continues his Gospel research with *The Gospel of St. Matthew* (CW 123). In January, his father dies. In April, he takes a month-long trip to Italy, including Rome, Monte Cassino, and Sicily. He also visits Scandinavia again. July–August, he writes the first mystery drama, *The Portal of Initiation* (CW 14). In November, he gives 'psychosophy' lectures. In December, he submits 'On the Psychological Foundations and Epistemological Framework of Theosophy' to the International Philosophical Congress in Bologna.

1911: The crisis in the Theosophical Society deepens. In January, 'The Order of the Rising Sun,' which will soon become 'The Order of the Star in the East,' is founded for the coming world teacher, Krishnamurti. At the same time, Marie von Sivers, Rudolf Steiner's co-worker, falls ill. Fewer lectures are given, but important new ground is broken. In Prague, in March, Steiner meets Franz Kafka (1883–1924) and Hugo Bergmann (1883-1975). In April, he delivers his paper to the Philosophical Congress. He writes the second mystery drama, *The Soul's Probation* (CW 14). Also, while Marie von Sivers is convalescing, Rudolf Steiner begins work on *Calendar 1912/1913*, which will contain the 'Calendar of the Soul' meditations. On March 19, Anna (Eunike) Steiner dies. In September, Rudolf Steiner visits Einsiedeln, birthplace of Paracelsus. In December, Friedrich Rittelmeyer, future founder of the Christian Community, meets Rudolf Steiner. The *Johannes-Bauverein*, the 'building committee,' which would lead to the first Goetheanum (first planned for Munich), is also founded, and a preliminary committee for the founding of an independent association is created that, in the following year, will become the Anthroposophical Society. Important lecture cycles include *Occult Physiology* (CW 128); *Wonders of the World* (CW 129); *From Jesus to Christ* (CW 131). Other themes: esoteric Christianity; Christian Rosenkreutz; the spiritual guidance of humanity; the sense world and the world of the spirit.

1912: Despite the ongoing, now increasing crisis in the Theosophical Society, much is accomplished: *Calendar 1912/1913* is published; eurythmy is created; both the third mystery drama, *The Guardian of the Threshold* (CW 14) and *A Way of Self-Knowledge* (CW 16) are written. New (or renewed) themes included life between death and rebirth and karma and reincarnation. Other lecture cycles: *Spiritual Beings in the Heavenly Bodies and in the Kingdoms of Nature* (CW 136); *The Human Being in the Light of Occultism, Theosophy, and Philosophy* (CW 137); *The Gospel of St. Mark* (CW 139); and *The Bhagavad Gita and the Epistles of Paul* (CW 142). On May 8, Rudolf Steiner celebrates White Lotus Day, H.P. Blavatsky's death day, which he had faithfully observed for the past decade, for the last time. In August, Rudolf Steiner suggests the 'independent association' be called the 'Anthroposophical Society.' In September, the first eurythmy course takes place. In October, Rudolf Steiner declines recognition of a Theosophical Society lodge dedicated to the Star of the East and decides to expel all Theosophical Society members belonging to the order. Also, with Marie von Sivers, he first visits Dornach, near Basel, Switzerland, and they stand on the hill where the Goetheanum will be built. In November, a Theosophical Society lodge is opened by direct mandate from Adyar (Annie Besant). In December, a meeting of the German section occurs at which it is decided that belonging to the Order of the Star of the East is incompatible with membership in the Theosophical Society. December 28: informal founding of the Anthroposophical Society in Berlin.

1913: Expulsion of the German section from the Theosophical Society. February 2–3: Foundation meeting of the Anthroposophical Society. Board members include: Marie von Sivers, Michael Bauer, and Carl Unger. September 20: Laying of the foundation stone for the *Johannes Bau* (Goetheanum) in Dornach. Building begins immediately. The third mystery drama, *The Soul's Awakening* (CW 14), is completed. Also: *The Threshold of the Spiritual World* (CW 147). Lecture cycles include: *The Bhagavad Gita and the Epistles of Paul* and *The Esoteric Meaning of the Bhagavad Gita* (CW 146), which the Russian philosopher Nikolai Berdyaev attends; *The Mysteries of the East and of Christianity* (CW 144); *The Effects of Esoteric Development* (CW 145); and *The Fifth Gospel* (CW 148). In May, Rudolf Steiner is in London and Paris, where anthroposophical work continues.

1914: Building continues on the *Johannes Bau* (Goetheanum) in Dornach, with artists and co-workers from seventeen nations. The general assembly of the Anthroposophical Society takes place. In May, Rudolf Steiner visits Paris, as well as Chartres Cathedral. June 28: assassination in Sarajevo ('Now the catastrophe has happened!'). August 1: War is declared. Rudolf Steiner returns to Germany from Dornach—he will travel back and forth. He writes the last chapter of *The Riddles of Philosophy*. Lecture cycles include: *Human and Cosmic Thought* (CW 151); *Inner Being of Humanity between Death and a New Birth* (CW 153); *Occult Reading and Occult Hearing* (CW 156). December 24: marriage of Rudolf Steiner and Marie von Sivers.

1915: Building continues. Life after death becomes a major theme, also art. Writes: *Thoughts during a Time of War* (CW 24). Lectures include: *The Secret of Death* (CW 159); *The Uniting of Humanity through the Christ Impulse* (CW 165).

1916: Rudolf Steiner begins work with Edith Maryon (1872–1924) on the sculpture 'The Representative of Humanity' ('The Group'—Christ, Lucifer, and Ahriman). He also works with the alchemist Alexander von Bernus on the quarterly *Das Reich*. He writes *The Riddle of Humanity* (CW 20). Lectures include: *Necessity and Freedom in World History and Human Action* (CW 166); *Past and Present in the Human Spirit* (CW 167); *The Karma of Vocation* (CW 172); *The Karma of Untruthfulness* (CW 173).

1917: Russian Revolution. The U.S. enters the war. Building continues. Rudolf Steiner delineates the idea of the 'threefold nature of the human being' (in a public lecture March 15) and the 'threefold nature of the social organism' (hammered out in May-June with the help of Otto von Lerchenfeld and Ludwig Polzer-Hoditz in the form of two documents titled *Memoranda*, which were distributed in high places). August–September: Rudolf Steiner writes *The Riddles of the Soul* (CW 20). Also: commentary on 'The Chymical Wedding of Christian Rosenkreutz' for Alexander Bernus (*Das Reich*). Lectures include: *The Karma of Materialism* (CW 176); *The Spiritual Background of the Outer World: The Fall of the Spirits of Darkness* (CW 177).

1918: March 18: peace treaty of Brest-Litovsk—'Now everything will truly enter chaos! What is needed is cultural renewal.' June: Rudolf Steiner visits Karlstein (Grail) Castle outside Prague. Lecture cycle: *From Symptom to Reality in Modern History* (CW 185). In mid-November, Emil Molt, of the Waldorf-Astoria Cigarette Company, has the idea of founding a school for his workers' children.

1919: Focus on the threefold social organism: tireless travel, countless lectures, meetings, and publications. At the same time, a new public stage of Anthroposophy emerges as cultural renewal begins. The coming years will see initiatives in pedagogy, medicine, pharmacology, and agriculture. January 27: threefold meeting: ' We must first of all, with the money we have, found free schools that can bring people what they need.' February: first public eurythmy performance in Zurich. Also: 'Appeal to the German People' (CW 24), circulated March 6 as a newspaper insert. In April, *Towards Social Renewal* (CW 23) appears— 'perhaps the most widely read of all books on politics appearing since the war.' Rudolf Steiner is asked to undertake the 'direction and leadership' of the school founded by the Waldorf-Astoria Company. Rudolf Steiner begins to talk about the 'renewal' of education. May 30: a building is selected and purchased for the future Waldorf School. August–September, Rudolf Steiner gives a lecture course for Waldorf teachers, *The Foundations of Human Experience (Study of Man)* (CW 293). September 7: Opening of the first Waldorf School. December (into January): first science course, the *Light Course* (CW 320).

1920: The Waldorf School flourishes. New threefold initiatives. Founding of limited companies *Der Kommende Tag* and *Futurum A.G.* to infuse spiritual values into the economic realm. Rudolf Steiner also focuses on the sciences. Lectures: *Introducing Anthroposophical Medicine* (CW 312); *The Warmth Course* (CW 321); *The Boundaries of Natural Science* (CW 322); *The Redemption of Thinking* (CW 74). February: Johannes Werner

Klein—later a co-founder of the Christian Community—asks Rudolf Steiner about the possibility of a 'religious renewal,' a 'Johannine church.' In March, Rudolf Steiner gives the first course for doctors and medical students. In April, a divinity student asks Rudolf Steiner a second time about the possibility of religious renewal. September 27–October 16: anthroposophical 'university course.' December: lectures titled *The Search for the New Isis* (CW 202).

1921: Rudolf Steiner continues his intensive work on cultural renewal, including the uphill battle for the threefold social order. 'University' arts, scientific, theological, and medical courses include: *The Astronomy Course* (CW 323); *Observation, Mathematics, and Scientific Experiment* (CW 324); the *Second Medical Course* (CW 313); *Colour*. In June and September–October, Rudolf Steiner also gives the first two 'priests' courses' (CW 342 and 343). The 'youth movement' gains momentum. Magazines are founded: *Die Drei* (January), and—under the editorship of Albert Steffen (1884–1963)—the weekly, *Das Goetheanum* (August). In February–March, Rudolf Steiner takes his first trip outside Germany since the war (Holland). On April 7, Steiner receives a letter regarding 'religious renewal,' and May 22–23, he agrees to address the question in a practical way. In June, the Klinical-Therapeutic Institute opens in Arlesheim under the direction of Dr. Ita Wegman. In August, the Chemical-Pharmaceutical Laboratory opens in Arlesheim (Oskar Schmiedel and Ita Wegman are directors). The Clinical Therapeutic Institute is inaugurated in Stuttgart (Dr. Ludwig Noll is director); also the Research Laboratory in Dornach (Ehrenfried Pfeiffer and Günther Wachsmuth are directors). In November–December, Rudolf Steiner visits Norway.

1922: The first half of the year involves very active public lecturing (thousands attend); in the second half, Rudolf Steiner begins to withdraw and turn toward the Society—'The Society is asleep.' It is 'too weak' to do what is asked of it. The businesses—*Der Kommende Tag* and *Futurum A.G.*—fail. In January, with the help of an agent, Steiner undertakes a twelve-city German lecture tour, accompanied by eurythmy performances. In two weeks he speaks to more than 2,000 people. In April, he gives a 'university course' in The Hague. He also visits England. In June, he is in Vienna for the East–West Congress. In August–September, he is back in England for the Oxford Conference on Education. Returning to Dornach, he gives the lectures *Philosophy, Cosmology, and Religion* (CW 215), and gives the third priests' course (CW 344). On September 16, The Christian Community is founded. In October–November, Steiner is in Holland and England. He also speaks to the youth: *The Youth Course* (CW 217). In December, Steiner gives lectures titled *The Origins of Natural Science* (CW 326), and *Humanity and the World of Stars: The Spiritual Communion of Humanity* (CW 219). December 31: Fire at the Goetheanum, which is destroyed.

1923: Despite the fire, Rudolf Steiner continues his work unabated. A very hard year. Internal dispersion, dissension, and apathy abound. There is conflict—between old and new visions—within the Society. A wake-up call is needed, and Rudolf Steiner responds with renewed lecturing vitality. His focus: the spiritual context of human life; initiation science; the course of the year; and community building. As a foundation for an artistic school, he creates a series of pastel sketches. Lecture cycles: *The Anthroposophical Movement; Initiation Science* (CW 227) (in England at the Penmaenmawr Summer School); *The Four Seasons and the Archangels* (CW 229); *Harmony of the Creative Word* (CW 230); *The Supersensible Human* (CW 231), given in Holland for the founding of the Dutch society. On November 10, in response to the failed Hitler-Ludendorff putsch in Munich, Steiner closes his Berlin residence and moves the *Philosophisch-Anthroposophisch Verlag* (Press) to Dornach. On December 9, Steiner begins the serialization of his *Autobiography: The Course of My Life* (CW 28) in *Das Goetheanum*. It will continue to appear weekly, without a break, until his death. Late December–early January: Rudolf Steiner refounds the Anthroposophical Society (about 12,000 members internationally) and takes over its leadership. The new board members are: Marie Steiner, Ita Wegman, Albert Steffen, Elisabeth Vreede, and Günther Wachsmuth. (See *The Christmas Meeting for the Founding of the General Anthroposophical Society*, CW 260). Accompanying lectures: *Mystery Knowledge and Mystery Centres* (CW 232); *World History in the Light of Anthroposophy* (CW 233). December 25: the Foundation Stone is laid (in the hearts of members) in the form of the 'Foundation Stone Meditation.'

1924: January 1: having founded the Anthroposophical Society and taken over its leadership, Rudolf Steiner has the task of 'reforming' it. The process begins with a weekly newssheet ('What's Happening in the Anthroposophical Society') in which Rudolf Steiner's 'Letters to Members' and 'Anthroposophical Leading Thoughts' appear (CW 26). The next step is the creation of a new esoteric class, the 'first class' of the 'University of Spiritual Science' (which was to have been followed, had Rudolf Steiner lived longer, by two more advanced classes). Then comes a new language for Anthroposophy—practical, phenomenological, and direct; and Rudolf Steiner creates the model for the second Goetheanum. He begins the series of extensive 'karma' lectures (CW 235–40); and finally, responding to needs, he creates two new initiatives: biodynamic agriculture and curative education. After the middle of the year, rumours begin to circulate regarding Steiner's health. Lectures: January–February, *Anthroposophy* (CW 234); February: *Tone Eurythmy* (CW 278); June: *The Agriculture Course* (CW 327); June–July: *Speech Eurythmy* (CW 279); *Curative Education* (CW 317); August: (England, 'Second International Summer School'), *Initiation Consciousness: True and False Paths in Spiritual Investigation* (CW 243); September: *Pastoral Medicine* (CW 318). On September 26, for the first time, Rudolf Steiner cancels a lecture. On September 28, he gives his last lecture. On September 29, he withdraws to his studio in the carpenter's shop; now he is definitively ill. Cared for by Ita Wegman, he continues working, however, and writing the weekly installments of his *Autobiography* and *Letters to the Members/Leading Thoughts* (CW 26).

1925: Rudolf Steiner, while continuing to work, continues to weaken. He finishes *Extending Practical Medicine* (CW 27) with Ita Wegman.
On March 30, around ten in the morning, Rudolf Steiner dies

INDEX

abstract/abstraction, 33–34, 51–52, 59–62, 75–79, 88, 104, 116, 118, 122–127, 131
absurdity, 4
'added value', 55, 66–67, 71–72, 79–80, 83–84
Adler-Unold Ethical Cultural Movement, 35
after-effects, 22
Ahriman/ahrimanic, 52, 79, 128–129
   Prince of this World, 26
America/American, 14
anthroposophical/Anthroposophy, 3–4, 24, 28, 32, 34–36, 38–39, 49–52, 54, 56–57, 59, 68–70, 74, 78–79, 89–90, 107, 109, 115, 117, 120–121, 129, 132, 134
anthroposophic movement, 13, 16, 28, 34, 51
anti-social, 65
antipathy, 91–92
Anzengruber, 93
appeal, 6–7, 11, 17, 54
'Appeal to the Civilized World', 5
archetypal/archetype, 99, 105
arithmetic, 44
arrogance, 4, 8
art/artistic, xi, 24, 26, 48, 57, 60, 65, 69, 91, 93–96, 125–126
   Expressionist, 61
   naturalistic, 63
   Impressionism, 60–61
aspirations, 1–2
assets, 112, 128

   economic assets, 112
   unfixed assets, 23
association/associative, 9, 23–24, 82, 85, 87, 128
astronomy, 70
atavistic, 35, 57, 61, 77
atheist, 29, 93
aura, 26
Austria, 6, 11, 14, 132
authenticity, 52
autonomy, 10
awareness, 3, 33, 100
   self-awareness, 125

balance, xi, 128–129
barbarism, 92
Basel, 4, 11, 15, 33, 37, 80, 83, 87–88
Berlin, 29
Berlin Workers' Association, 52
Bern/Bernese, 2–4, 11, 14–15, 97, 107–108, 113, 115–116
Bolshevik/Bolshevism, 14, 37, 43, 72–73, 122
   Russian, 73
Boos, Dr, 2, 5, 16, 54
bourgeois/bourgeoisie, 2, 42–48, 51–52, 61–62, 64, 66–69, 133
breathing, 109–110
bureaucracy, 43–44, 49, 104
   as 'military machinery', 43, 49

cameralistic, 49
capital/capitalism, xii, 22, 33, 39–41, 44, 49, 51, 66, 78, 98,

102–105, 109–111, 113, 118, 128
capital assets, 44
capital interest, 22
carbon dioxide, 109
Catholic, 70
  Church, 115, 133
chaos/chaotic, x, 4, 17, 101, 134
charlatanism, 89, 104
chemistry, 53
Christ, 29–31, 61–62, 107, 115
  Christ mystery, 61
  'Son of the living God', 107, 115
Christian/Christianity, xi, 29–30, 62, 93, 97–98, 104, 114–115
  Christian era, 61
  Christianized, 97
Church, 26, 34
clairvoyance, atavistic, 114
clarity, xii
class (social), 2, 9
  class conflict, 72
  class consciousness, 63–64, 67, 72, 78
  class warfare, 55, 71
  middle class, 74, 96
  ruling class, 2, 18, 20, 94
  working class, 2, 18, 33, 63, 95
'cliquish', 69
cognition, 51
collectives, 9
comets, 70
comfort, 6
commodity, xii, 80–82, 99–101, 112
communal bodies, 9
communications, 4, 6, 39
Communism, 48
community, 14, 21, 24–25, 33, 40, 76, 79, 83, 128
  commonality, 113
    'commonality of all', 40
  religious, 25
  social, 9, 14, 22, 45

concept, 24, 28, 58–60, 114, 125, 128
concrete, 34
confusion, 22
conscious/consciousness, 9, 55–57, 62–64, 67, 69, 71–72, 80
  class consciousness, 63–64, 67, 72, 78
  state consciousness, 63
  subconscious, 20, 27, 35, 56, 62, 65, 71–72, 80, 132
  unconscious, 35, 55, 57–59, 134
consciousness soul, 55, 57, 59
  era, 65, 114, 131
contemplate/contemplation, 8–9, 11, 98
contract, 83
cooperatives, 9, 23
copyright, 112
cosmic/cosmos, 4, 114
countenance, 60
courage, 12
creation, 124
credit transfers, 100
cultural/culture, xi, 25–27, 31, 49–50, 59, 66–67, 71, 77, 94–95, 102–104, 113, 117, 121
  cultural life, 56–57, 68, 70, 83, 86, 91–92, 102–103
  German culture, 7
currency value, 101
custodianship, 112

death/death principle, 50-51
delectation, 66
democracy/democratic, 37, 47, 63, 102
Democrat (American), 14
desperate, 6
destiny, 1, 6, 25–26
digestive system, 82
dignity, 95
disaster, 121, 133

distinctive forces, 3
distortion, 32
dogma, 3
dream/dreaming, 87–89
dreamers, 16

ecclesiasticism, 133
echo, 25
economics/economy, x–xii, 8, 10, 14,
    22, 25–26, 33–34, 39, 44,
    49–50, 56–57, 62–63, 67–68,
    71, 77, 80–84, 91–92, 98,
    100–102, 112, 121, 128
  economic asset, 112
  economic cycle, 111–112
  economic forces, 5
  economic life, 9, 17, 23, 27–28, 50,
    54, 56–57, 61–62, 66–68, 78,
    81–86, 92, 99, 101–102,
    104–105, 118
  economic order, 33–34, 52
  economic professors, 99
  necessary economics, 90
educate/education, xi, 22, 26, 31,
    67–68, 91, 94–95
egoism/egoistic, 18, 30, 65–67, 72
Egypt, 58
Eisner, Kurt, 87–88
emotion/emotional, 3, 5, 53
enforcement, 49
England, 40, 99
Engles, 40
equality, xi, 45–46, 68
  inequality, 45–46
equilibrium, 129–130
ethical/ethics, xi, 18, 34–35, 130–131
evil, 78–79
  evil spirit, 87
'Ex deo nascimur', 29, 31
expression, 129
  manifest expression, 129
Expressionist. *See art/artistic,
    Expressionist*

fable, 54
fable convenue, 54
factional/factionalism, 35, 51
facts, 6, 88
faith, x, 49, 62, 114
  blind faith, 49–50, 62
  superstitious faith, 49
faithful, 107
fanatical, 41
fantasy, 15–16, 81, 104
  fantasist, 16, 18, 38, 99, 103
Farmers' Federation, 85
feel/feeling, xi, 2, 18, 21, 29–32, 56,
    63, 65, 70, 80, 88, 93–94,
    98–99, 108, 113–114, 120
  feeling phases, 92
  instinctive feeling, 21
  middle-class feeling, 63
  social feeling, 49
Fichte, Johann G, 72–73, 75–78,
    121–122
  Closed Commercial State, The, 73, 75,
    122
  Theory of Knowledge, 76
formative forces, 114
forms, 9, 12, 26, 37, 54, 97, 118, 123
  book-form, 54
  thought-form, 42
foundation, xii, 3, 6, 13, 24, 27–28,
    35–36, 40, 50, 54, 67, 74, 84,
    92, 103, 117, 123, 127, 131,
    133
France/French, 38, 43
fraternity, xi, 27
free/freedom, 14, 21, 32, 49, 56, 86,
    130
  freedom in thinking (thought), 62,
    64–65, 68, 72
  unfree, 32
fruitfulness, 102

gentrified/gentry, 18, 33–34, 52–53,
    65, 67, 69

gentry egoism, 67
gentry outlook, 18
German/Germany, 2, 5–8, 10–12, 14, 20, 40, 106
  German Revolution, 116
Gladstone, 133
God, 29, 31, 34, 52, 62, 93, 98, 123–124, 126–127
  Father God, 31
  living God, 107, 115, 123
Goethe
  Faust, Part II, 73
gold, 99–100
goods, 81–82, 84
Gospels, 29, 115
government, 9
Graz University, 107
Greek, 58, 77
ground rent, xii, 22–24, 39, 84

hard-heartedness, 47
harmonious/harmony, x, 10, 75
Harnack, 29
  Nature of Christianity, The, 29
head system, xi, 9–10, 32, 74, 114–115, 122
heal/healing, 3–4, 52, 79, 88, 98, 105, 111, 117
  healing impulse, 79
  healing powers, 4
heart, xi, 18, 20, 54, 82
Hebrew, ancient, 113
Hegel/Hegelian, 38, 77, 122–131
  Encyclopedia of the Philosophical Sciences, 122
historical/history, 2, 13, 54, 56–58, 61, 67, 71–78, 106, 125, 134
homunculus, 74
honesty, 52
hope, 14
human
  as animal creature, 130–131
  human rights, 109

humility, 4
hypotheses, 5

I (ego), 75–76
  not-I, 76
'I am with you, even unto the end of the world', 30
idea, x, xii, 1, 17–18, 28, 30, 58–59, 62, 89, 99, 106, 114–115, 122–131
ideal, 12, 15
idealism/idealist, 8, 16, 30–31, 34, 127–128, 130
ideologically/ideology, 16, 49–50, 57–58, 77, 117–118
  'surface ideology', x–xi
'Ignorabimus', 43, 48
ignorance, 48
illusion, 52, 82
image, 9, 58, 77
  mirror-image, 57
imagination, 58–59, 79, 87, 114
implementation, 15
impotence, 59
impoverishment, 14
impression, 5, 15, 60–61
Impressionist. *See art/artistic, Impressionist*
impulses, 2, 32, 53, 55–56, 71, 78, 114–115
  dead impulse, 115
  social impulse, 80
  soul impulse, 55
'Inasmuch as you have done it to the least of my brethren, ye have done it unto me', 30
income (monetary), 21
incorporate, 35
individuality, 25, 65
initiatives, 9, 62
inspiration, 58
instincts, 4, 13, 56, 98
institutions, 8, 19

'International Revolutionary Social
    Democracy', 64
internationalism, 64
    proletariat, 64
intuition, 57–58, 114
Intuition (stage), 130
inwardness, 91

Jagow, 106
Jesuitical, 107
'Jesuology', 61
Jesus (of Nazareth), 61–62, 107
    as 'simple man of Nazareth', 62
judge/judgment, 1, 6, 13, 25, 56, 113
    professional, 62
justice, 27
justification, 10

Kaiser, 64
    'Three Cheers for the Kaiser', 64
Kant, 130
karma, 1, 25–26, 65, 92–93, 113
knowledge, 18, 58, 117
    self-knowledge, 56
    spiritual knowledge, 71
    spiritual-scientific knowledge, 51,
        117
Kuhn, Herr, 2, 5, 54

labour, xii, 9, 23, 33, 45, 48, 51, 55,
    63, 66–67, 80, 82–84, 90,
    103–104, 112
land, 22–23, 112
language, 3–4, 92, 94, 96–98, 112
Lasalle, 46
law, 9–10, 21, 24–25, 27, 62, 113, 125
    Boyle-Mariotte law, 23
    civil law, 47
    criminal law, 24
    lawfulness, 21, 24
    mortgage law, 22
    private law, 24
    realty-attuned law, 30

l' decadence, 96
League of Nations (Conference),
    106–107, 115–116, 118–120
legal, xi, 90
    legal regulation, 91
legislature, 17
Lenin, Vladimir, x, 38–48, 50, 72
    State and Revolution, The, 46
liberal, 37
liberty, xi
lie, 29, 31, 80, 83, 94
    untruth, 80, 82
life of rights, 83, 85
life of spirit, 49–50
limbs, xi
logic, 122–126, 129, 131
logical reasoning, 31
London, 38
love, 28, 93, 97–98
loyalty, 38
Lucifer/luciferic, 52, 128
Ludendorff, General, 16
lung and heart system. See *rhythmic
    system*
lungs, 9

manifesto, 6
Marx, Karl/Marxists, x, 38–42, 45–47,
    122, 127–130
    as 'social chauvinists', 40
material life, 93
materialism/materialistic, x–xi, 28, 38,
    55–57, 62, 67, 71, 78, 97, 109,
    127–129
    ahrimanic materialism, 128
    historical materialism, 78
    materialistic forces, 8
    materialistic Jesus, 62
mathematics, 53, 108
Mauthner, Fritz, 89–90
    Dictionary of Philosophy, 89
mechanics, 124
medicine, 117

mentality, 63
metamorphoses. *See transform/transformation*
mindlessness, 88
minds, 20, 128
mirroring, 91, 122
misery, x, 14
misfortune, 54
modernism/modernity, 69–70, 133
money, 98–101
  monetary, 105
moral/morality, 28, 52, 104, 130
  imagination, 130
  life, 61
  philosophy, 130
  renewal, 35
Mott, Herr, 2, 5, 54
mummified, 12–13, 37
mystic/mysticism, xii, 77

narrow-mindedness, 8
National Assembly (Weimar), 109, 116–117
naturalism/naturalistic, 60–61
nature, 124–126, 128, 130–131
new world order, 13, 97
Nicholas II, Tzar, 133

objective, 1, 54
observation/observe, 4, 12–13, 20, 24
Old Testament, 29, 31
opinions, of others, 31
oppressive, 109
originality, xii
ownership, 112
oxygen, 109–110

Palestine, 62
Paris, 2–4, 96
peace, 33, 119–120
perceive/perception, xi, 34, 51, 60, 77, 88–89, 93, 116, 122, 134
pessimistic, 3

philosophical/philosophy, 32, 54, 63, 73, 76, 124–127, 129, 131
Philosophy of Freedom, The, 130
physics, 23, 53
pictorial, 58–59, 124
pity, 16
Pobedonostsev, 133
political/politics, 9–10, 14, 17, 24, 26–27, 31, 37, 50, 68, 82–84, 112
  political life, 68, 85, 99, 104, 112
  political state, 117
ponder, 35, 127
positivism, 38
post Atlantean Cultural Eras
  1st (Ancient Indian), 57–58
  2nd (Ancient Persian), 58
  3rd (Egyptian/Chaldean), 58
  4th (Greco-Roman), 58–59
  5th (Present), 36, 59
potentiality, 10
power, 89
practical/practicality, 8
pragmatism/pragmatist, 8, 11, 16, 59, 88–89, 106
precedent, 2
preconception, 13, 20, 29–31, 58
precondition, 27
prejudice, 13–14, 29–31
  unprejudiced, 8
pride, 8
principalities, 116
principles, xi
production/productivity, 9, 22, 128
  cultural, 10
  spiritual, 10
profit, 56
proletarian/proletariat, 2, 18, 33, 38–43, 45–47, 52–53, 55–56, 61–64, 66–68, 71–72, 76, 82, 94, 99, 117
  movement, 71–72, 77, 109
  revolution, 79

property, private, 111
proposal, 13–14
Protestant, 62
psyche, 113
psychology, 113
Pythagoras, 24, 132
   'Theorem of Pythagoras', 53

radicalism, 72
Raphael, 131
   'Sistine Madonna', 94, 131–132
rational, 12
Rauscher, Cardinal, 133
raw materials, 23
reactionary, 51
reality, x, 1–3, 5–6, 11–16, 18–19,
      21–24, 31, 38–39, 42–43,
      49–51, 56–57, 59–60, 67–68,
      71, 73, 76, 78, 80, 84, 87–89,
      92, 96–97, 102, 104–106,
      108, 110, 115–120, 124,
      126–128, 130–131, 133–134
   distorted, 31
   dreamed, 87, 95
   perceived, xii
realist, 128
realization, 12, 14, 20, 35, 116
   sense, 59–60
rebirth, inner, 29
redemption, 28
reflection, 2
   self-reflecting, 7
reform, xii
religion/religious, xi, 18, 24, 57, 61, 91,
      93, 98, 107, 125–126
   religiosity, 34
remuneration, 19, 56, 82
res publica, 90
respiratory system, 10, 82
rhythm, xi
rhythmic system, 74, 82
Ricardo, 39
rights, xi, 47, 81–84, 102

life of rights, 82–83, 85–86
rights sphere, 112
Romans, 77
Russia, 40

salvation, 31, 121
Schelling, 77
schismatic, 34, 51
Scholastics, 77
Schücking, 116
science, 24, 43, 52–53, 56, 74, 91, 114
sectarianism, 35, 51
self
   self-deception, 52
   self-examination, 7
   self-reflection, 7
sense/sensory, 57, 59–60, 74, 78, 125,
      127, 129
sense-perceptible, 61
sensibility, 97
Sermon on the Mount, 97
sermonizer/sermonizing, xi, 97, 104
Shylock/Shylockian, 47
Sistine Madonna. *See Raphael, Sistine*
      Madonna
slave/slavery, 34, 51
social/sociological, xi, 1–2, 13, 17–18,
      27, 31, 36–37, 39, 43–44, 54,
      121
   armed workers, 43–44
   cancer/carcinoma, 89, 96
   classes, 2, 9
   conditions, 17, 22
   context, 88
   demands, 8
   democracy, 14
   dynamics, xi
   form/reform, xii
   impulse, 18, 31, 72
   insight, 18, 21, 37
   instincts, 9
   labour, 9
   mechanism, 32

movement, 3, 50, 56, 71, 78
order, 45, 48, 110
positivism, 38
'social chauvinists', 40
socialization, 9, 45, 48, 104, 128
structure, 9–10
understanding, 17–18, 36–37
Social Democrat, 64
social organism (threefold), 9–10, 14, 19–25, 28, 30, 33–37, 39, 51–52, 65–66, 68, 73–75, 79–81, 83–86, 91, 93, 95, 98, 101–105, 108–113, 117, 121
  cultural/spiritual, 10, 19–20, 24, 26–27, 66, 68, 74, 102, 117–118
  economic, 10, 19–20, 25–27, 39, 74, 91, 101–102
  political, 9–10, 19–20, 24, 26–27, 37, 68, 74, 83–84, 101–102
  threefolding, xi, 19–20, 24–25, 27–28, 35–37, 39, 51, 54, 73, 75, 83–84, 86, 101, 111
socialism/socialist, 37–40, 43–52, 56, 65, 67–68, 72–73, 97, 109, 121, 129, 134
  radical socialism, 72
  socialist ideal, 74, 79
  socialist thinking, 73–74
  socialist world order, 79
Socialist Congress (Bern), 3, 14
society, x–xi, 1, 3–4, 9, 18–19, 28, 33, 74, 110, 112–113
soul
  impulses, 55
  realm, 90
speech, 92
spending, 85
spirit, 93, 95, 97–98, 103–105, 114, 117–118, 121, 126, 129–130
  spirit land (world), 91–92
spiritual, 4–5, 10, 25–26, 35, 49, 77, 93, 96, 105, 113, 115, 131

cognition, 49
culture, 97
forces, 4
impulse, 5, 49, 127
insight, 71
life, 34, 56, 68, 77, 83, 86, 90, 92–93, 99, 102–103, 118, 128
movement, 69
sphere, 33
spirituality, 24, 26, 121–122, 128, 130
  unspirituality, 14
spiritualized, 127
world, 130–131
spiritual science. *See Anthroposophy/ anthroposophical*
status nascens, 113
Stein, Herr, 11
Steiner, Rudolf
  Philosophy of Freedom, The, 130
  Riddles of Philosophy, 58, 75, 127
  Theosophy, 90–91
  'To the German People and the Civilized World', 7
Stuttgart, 2
sub-human, as, 27
suffer, xi
supersensible, 27, 57, 120, 125–127, 129, 131
superstition/superstitious, 49–50, 73–74
  alchemical superstition, 74
  superstitious faith, 49
suppression, 47
Switzerland (Swiss), 1, 6, 11–13
sympathy, 91–92

tax system/taxation, xii, 19–20, 84–86, 101
theologian/theology, 29, 31, 117
theosophy, 68–69
  theosophical movement, 51, 68–69
thinking/thoughts, xi–xii, 4–6, 8–9,

11, 13, 15–16, 18, 21, 24, 29–32, 36–43, 45, 50–54, 56–57, 61–62, 65, 67, 74–78, 81, 8, 90, 98–99, 107–110, 114–121, 124, 127, 132
  abstract, 76–79, 114, 127
  Bolshevik, 76
  bourgeois, 2, 52
  conceptual, 59
  dead, 109, 115
  destructive, 79
  energetic, 77
  Fichtean, 75, 77, 79
  higher, 27
  idealistic, 127
  materialistic, 127
  modern, 89, 129
  mummified, 13
  pure, 75–77, 129
  reality-friendly, 117–118, 120
  social/socialistic, xii, 43, 73, 80, 109, 117, 119, 121, 127, 129
  spiritual, 129
  spiritual science, 38, 89
  spiritually oriented, 114
  subjective, 122
  supersensible, 31
  suppressed, 132
  thought-form, 42, 44
  tripartite, xi
thinking, feeling, will, 36
threefold/threefolding. *See social organism, threefolding*
time (in understanding life), 110–111
token value, 101
tolerance, inner, 30
transform/transformation, 9, 31, 36, 44, 72, 78, 109, 111, 114–115, 121, 128
triangles, 24
trinity, modern, 128
Trotsky, 72–73
true/truth, 9, 52–53, 55, 72, 80, 97, 104, 121, 128
untruth, 31, 80, 82
trust, 86, 103, 105
turning points, 12

Ude, Prof., 107–108
understanding, 4–5, 12, 17–18, 20–22, 28, 30–31, 36–37, 51, 71, 86, 104
  logical, 31
  reciprocal, 103
  social, 20–22, 31
Unger, Dr, 54
unifying, 64
unity, 64
unknowingness, 43
utopia/utopian, 15–16, 87

'vale of tears', 114
Vienna/Viennese, 11, 89, 96
violation, 82
  economic, 82
vitality, 134

wages, xi, 39, 79, 84, 101
Wagner, 74
Weimar, 109, 116–117
well-worn tracks, 106–107, 109
will/willing, xi, 5, 8, 16, 18, 20, 30–31, 36, 55, 74
Wilson, Woodrow (US President), 13, 32, 115–116, 119
wither/withering, 47–48
Wolf, 63
  'On the Nature of the Human Soul', 63
  his 'pre-Kantian philosophy', 63
world order, new, 13, 97
worldview, 2, 104, 107–108
  materialistic, 109

Yahweh, 29

Zurich, 4, 11, 15–16, 54

A note from Rudolf Steiner Press

We are an independent publisher and registered charity (non-profit organisation) dedicated to making available the work of Rudolf Steiner in English translation. We care a great deal about the content of our books and have hundreds of titles available – as printed books, ebooks and in audio formats.

As a publisher devoted to anthroposophy...

- We continually commission translations of previously unpublished works by Rudolf Steiner and invest in re-translating, editing and improving our editions.

- We are committed to making anthroposophy available to all by publishing introductory books as well as contemporary research.

- Our new print editions and ebooks are carefully checked and proofread for accuracy, and converted into all formats for all platforms.

- Our translations are officially authorised by Rudolf Steiner's estate in Dornach, Switzerland, to whom we pay royalties on sales, thus assisting their critical work.

So, look out for Rudolf Steiner Press as a mark of quality and support us today by buying our books, or contact us should you wish to sponsor specific titles or to support the charity with a gift or legacy.

office@rudolfsteinerpress.com
Join our e-mailing list at www.rudolfsteinerpress.com

RUDOLF STEINER PRESS